Be aware of wonder, live a balanced life,
learn some and think some and draw and
paint and sew and sing and dance and play
and work every day some.
Robert Fulghum

Creating with Fabric

A TweetyJill Publication

by Jill Haglund

Previous Page:
Aware of Wonder
*The keyword in the quote was "sew". I searched though my photo
collection to find an image of someone sewing, preferably a child because
of the "dance and play" reference. Sometimes when I put together a
particularly wonderful Fragment I will dance around the room with joy.
It's all a part of keeping the wonder alive. ~ Lesley Riley*

ACKNOWLEDGEMENTS

Published and created by:
TweetyJill Publications, Inc.
5824 Bee Ridge Road, PMB 412
Sarasota, FL 34233
For information about wholesale,
please contact customer service at
www.tweetyjill.com or 1-800-595-5497.

*TweetyJill Publications, Inc. has taken every measure to ensure that all infor-
mation in this book is accurate. In addition, since individual skill levels, tools
and circumstances vary, we cannot be held responsible for any losses, injuries
or damages that may result from using any information provided in this book.*

Printed in China
ISBN 1-891898-13-6

Book Layout: Jill Haglund

Graphic Designer: Laurie Doherty

Creative Director: Jill Haglund

Managing Editor: Lisa Codianne Fowler

Photography: Herb Booth
of Herb Booth Studios, Inc., Sarasota, FL

Photo Stylist: Jill Haglund and Lindsay Haglund

Table of Contents

We don't want to forget buttons!

Much of the fabric artwork contains gorgeous vintage buttons. If you never had a reason to buy those beautiful buttons before - now you do. This is a hobby as easy and fun, as it is addictive! Start collecting right away for "Creating with Fabric" projects. Shop eBay, antique stores, flea markets, garage and estate sales—even consider your grandma's attic. ~ Jill Haglund

Make the Move from Paper to Fabric!

It's easy with "Creating with Fabric" by TweetyJill Publications

Transcend beyond the realm of paper and treat your senses to FABRIC — a multi-dimensional medium that begs to be explored! The touch, look and feel of it presents possibilities you never before imagined. Its no wonder fabric has fast become the medium of choice for artists and crafters alike.

Once you wrap your mind around fabric, a kaleidoscope of ideas will swirl around your head. And then the challenge…where to begin? This book will show you. Learn and be inspired by well-known international artists such as KC Willis, Lesley Riley, Pamela Allen, Lisa Engelbrecht, Julie McCullough, and myself, Jill Haglund.

Beautiful, detailed photographs along with step-by-step instructions help you successfully create fabric treasures; give them to family and friends as lifetime keepsakes.

KC Willis, our real-life cowgirl from Colorado, shares the techniques behind her incredible artwork - multiple layers, burnt/ scorched edges, decorative stitching and dozens of other innovative ideas.

See Lesley Riley's new Fragments as well as her latest Journal Fragments, learn her photo transfer and photo aging secrets through illustrative photos. See a first-time sampling of artwork from her students and how she inspires and encourages every artist!

Pamela Allen, award-winning journal quilter, shares her best. Her attention to detail and background scenes within each quilt are spellbinding. Her wit and fabulous stories accompany each spectacular piece.

Discover the skills and learn about the unique materials multimedia artist Lisa Engelbrecht uses to express her calligraphic lettering on fabric; and Deb Lewis's colorful, beaded dolls will simply make you smile.

Personally, I thoroughly enjoy the time spent in the creative process of fabric work. Inspired by KC Willis and Lesley Riley in Chapter 11, I made fabric pieces with minimal sewing and teeming with embellishments. As a die-hard, passionate vintage button and photograph collector, I utilize both in most of my fabric art.

This is a small sampling of visual treats and hands-on learning experiences from just a few of the artists featured in "Creating with Fabric". Such amazing talent and fabulous art in one book doesn't come along every day.

Take your time, peruse the pages, pick your projects… and enjoy!

Jill Haglund
TweetyJill Publications
Founder

CHAPTER 1

MATERIALS

A common thread woven through the soul of all fabric artists is the love of texture, color, dimension and energy that fabric brings to a project. With just some basic materials on hand, you can complete nearly every beautiful piece presented in this book and embrace firsthand, the "fabric of life".

If you already sew, you will be familiar with and probably already own everything listed on the following page... a sewing machine with decorative stitch capability, swatches and more swatches of favorite fabrics, spools and spools of colorful thread and scissors. Some fabric artists like using a rotary cutter and mat for straight, accurate cuts. Of course, you'll also need a ruler or tape measure, needles, seam ripper and a pin cushion.

An important word about scissors... don't cut yourself short! Purchase a quality pair of fabric shears such as Mundial or Fiskars. They are worth every penny, sharp and always ready to do what you expect. Make sure they are specifically designed for fabric cutting, and once you own them, do not use them on paper as this will dull their edges. Each year, have them sharpened at your local fabric store. Keep them with your sewing items and only use them for cutting material.

Optionally, it's nice to have a small pair of scissors to snip hanging threads as you pull from the sewing machine or that are bothersome once your piece is completed.

At the same time, keep in mind that fabrics do not have to be cut straight nor every thread snipped; I believe a good part of the beauty is the raw edges - the imperfect cuts and pulled thread edges. Lesley Riley calls it the "spontaneity of the work".

You will need to have plenty of bobbins filled with thread in a rainbow of colors that are ready to switch out when sewing; buy at least a dozen extra bobbins and fill with the colors you sew with most often. Always have them on hand.

What I personally love most about the projects in "Creating with Fabric" is the initial process of "sorting through your stash" and then the final selection of coordinating fabrics; I truly savor this creative part. I also relish juxtaposing layers of fabrics and literally "playing" until I'm pleased with the results. I don't do this hastily. I deliberately take my time, in the same manner I would delight in chatting and sipping tea with an old friend. Learn to enjoy the process of fabric art; the colors, textures, balance.

Sometimes, just for a change, I actually have a color wheel out when choosing fabric patterns (although I pretty much have a color wheel in my head). If you are new to the idea of matching fabrics, this may aid you in choosing your colors. Keep in mind that more interesting and striking projects come from unexpected color, fabric and pattern combinations.

Whether you are a novice to fabric art or have been sewing for years, "Creating with Fabric" will introduce you to a tapestry of new ideas for this coveted, centuries-old art form.

Jill Haglund's Studio

CHAPTER 2

Meet the Artists

We are honored to have the pleasure of introducing you to some of the world's most renowned fabric artists. The following pages contain a behind-the-scenes look at what makes them tick! In rare interviews, these great women get up close and personal, taking us beyond their artwork and into their lives.

Lesley Riley not only shares the secrets behind her famous Fragments, but describes her mission in life. Her inspiration and influence extends to a number artists featured in this book: Kristen Robinson, Deb Lewis and Amy Hahn. KC Willis delivers insights, humorous to heartwarming, that explain who she is today. Lisa Englebrecht gets to the heart of her motivations while Julie takes us back to her childhood. Pamela Allen makes us laugh as she speaks candidly about middle-age.

These artists warmly welcome us into their homes and their studios. Sit back, relax and enjoy a day in the life of each.

Julie McCullough's Studio

Lesley Riley's Studio

Pamela Allen's Studio

Meet KC Willis

Lisa Engelbrecht's Studio

CHAPTER 3 LESLEY RILEY

"There's magic in art. Making art makes us happy. Creating fulfills the eternal longing of the soul. Our soul craves expression. Art is the soul made visible. I create and show my art so that others can get to know the real me. Through my art I hope to inspire others and share the magic."

Author, columnist, editor, teacher, wife, mother, real estate appraiser… Lesley Riley wears many hats, but the feather in the cap she covets most is creating and inspiring art. Best known for her Fragment Series of small fabric collages, Lesley is an internationally known artist, art quilter and doll maker with a passion for color and the written word. Her art and articles have appeared in numerous books and magazines; she is Contributing Editor of the magazine, *Cloth Paper Scissors*, has two published books, "Quilted Memories" and "Fabric Memory Books" and a DVD, "Exploring Fabric Collage". She teaches an array of mixed-media workshops throughout the country and around the world.

And no matter the media or meeting place, her message is constant and clear: "If I can do it, you can do it!"

She doesn't have much time, a lot of space, nor a formal art education degree, circumstances that she is quick to reveal to illustrate her point. She works as a real estate appraiser with her husband (and childhood sweetheart); she's raised six children and has four grandchildren. Since spending time with her family is a priority, Lesley has always created her famous artwork at home.

"My studio is in my bedroom," she explains. "Leaving the house wasn't an option because I'd probably never come home. So I work where I am – I started in the basement but everyone was upstairs. I wanted to be where they were. I literally "worked my way up".

Her days are masterpieces of multitasking. "Every day I get up and I think, today I'm going to get a lot of art done, and I've been thinking this for years. The first thing I do is get my youngest off to school, then answer e-mails and online stuff. I usually don't get into my studio until after noon. I'll be working on several projects at once; I usually have five deadlines every month. If I get stuck, I'll do some Fragments because they are like a warm-up exercise for me. I work until it's time to cook dinner, because I'm still an old-fashioned housewife, then go back and work until probably 9:00 at night."

Going to "work" means creating as many as 500 Fragments a year, to date, thousands of the recognizable 8" x 10" multi-dimensional pieces, in addition to a myriad of other creations. The fabrics she uses come from "anywhere and everywhere": online shopping, estate sales, garage sales and fabric stores wherever she travels. Her studio is a goldmine of colors and textures. "I've been accumulating these over the years – I have a huge stash." For a beginner, she warns, it can get quite expensive, so she suggests rethinking old clothes and going to garage sales ("head for the basement for vintage finds"). For Lesley, whether there are financial limitations or time constraints, where there is passion, there is a path. And she's made it her mission to be a guiding light to help others find their way.

Create Wonder!
Lesley Riley

"When you have multiple obligations, children or not – when you're not a full-time artist, it's hard to work art into your life," she acknowledges. "So I've spent many years trying to do that, and just want to share it with people. To me, nothing is worth it unless you can get art done. I get very cranky if I can't! Ever since I started doing this it's rare that I am, which has helped my husband accept this because he sees how genuinely happy I am, even if I 'ditch' him and leave town for ten days!"

The native and resident of Bethesda, Maryland, has used her journeys for personal growth while inspiring others to find their own voice and create their art.

It's "serious fun", she says, and advises it shouldn't be stressful. "There's a point where you might be trying something new so you're a little scared or anxious, but in the long run it's got to be fun. I use photographs, that's what I enjoy doing. You've got to find the technique that makes you feel good."

Lesley found hers back in 2000 when an ice storm knocked out the power to her home. "I was trying to find my own voice in art, and what is it I wanted to do. I had done quilting, baskets, weaving, watercolor, oil painting and really didn't know what I was doing. So, I interviewed myself. What is it about other people's art that I'm drawn to? I loved photographs and text; I loved quotes and had been collecting them since I was a teenager. And I loved collages, so I started using those limited daylight hours to make Fragments – fragments of fabric and fragments of art."

Lesley still makes it up as she goes; her work is totally spontaneous. Learn more about her and her art at www.LaLasLand.com. Why LaLas Land? "When my sister and I were children, she couldn't pronounce "Lesley". LaLa became my nickname, and my Dad, and later, my husband picked up on it. Go to my website – visit LaLas Land. It's my alter ego. The picture - the little girl - that's me."

No matter how young or old you are, Lesley says, it's never too late. Having discovered her own inner voice in her late 30's, she muses, "I got this all 'late' in life. What if I never tapped into it? Never discovered I could do this? I just want to make sure a lot of people find out they CAN do it. You've just got to work it into your schedule. Just do it. Spend some time with art discovering what you have to say."

CHAPTER 4

Fragment Series How-To
❧ Lesley Riley ❧

When Leslie does her "Fragments Series" she prints her quotes and photographs onto fabric. Below are the instructions to make a fragment.

MATERIALS

FABRICS: Various Fabrics; Prepared Fabric by ColorTextiles

OTHER: Pellon Wonder Under; Scanned Photo or images on CDs from www.LalasLand.com by Lesley Riley

TOOLS: Iron; Bernina Sewing Machine; Pins; Photoshop by Adobe (or other photo editing software); Scissors

PRINTER: Epson C88 printer with DURA-Brite Inks

INSTRUCTIONS

PRINTING PHOTOS ONTO FABRIC

1. Scan photo into your computer, download photo from your camera, or use an image from a photo collection CD.

2. Enhance photo quality using functions of software. I often increase contrast, brighten, increase color saturation for richer looking color images, or decrease saturation for a sepia-toned effect. Enlarge, reduce or crop to desired size.

3. Using paper-backed fabric prepared for inkjet printing (ColorTextiles, EQ Printables), follow manufacturer's instructions and print image onto fabric. (Note: In your photo editing program, fill a page with several images before printing to get the most out of your fabric.)

4. Remove fabric from paper backing and iron onto Wonder Under. Cut out photos. (Wonder Under prevents edges from fraying.)

5. Using word processing software, type quotes. Follow steps 3 and 4 and print quotes onto inkjet ready fabric.

6. Choose fabrics to complement and reinforce message in photo. Select a large background fabric and several smaller ones to frame photo and create interest. Tuck small snippets of contrasting colors or textures behind the photo to add punch or eye candy to the piece.

10. When you have an arrangement you like, pin everything in place. To prevent layers from slipping when sewing, place fusible interfacing behind each of the larger pieces of fabric (not the small snippets). Cut fusible interfacing to a size smaller than the fabric you are placing it behind and tuck it underneath the fabric. When all of the fabric pieces have Wonder Under behind them, iron the entire piece. Make sure that there is no exposed Wonder Under to come in contact with your iron.

8. Machine-stitch fused Fragment. No need to take it apart and sew from the bottom up. Just stitch the exposed areas of each piece of fabric. Fabric snippets will be held down by stitching over the top of the fabric they are tucked under.

CHAPTER 5

Fragment Gallery

I collect quotes, photos and fabric separately. It's when I sit down to create that they all come together to tell a complete story, each element mirroring or magnifying the others. Sometimes I will start with the photo and find fabrics to set the mood. Other times, with quote in hand, I will go searching for a photo to illustrate the wisdom of the words. And of course, there are days when I just want to play with combining beautiful colors and fabrics and I will find a photo to top them off.
~ Lesley Riley

It is a happy talent to know how to play.
Ralph Waldo Emerson

How to Play

This pale tinted vintage photo needed some dressing up. I chose a graphic red checked homespun and accented it with bright orange silk and a shock of purple. The pattern in the vintage bark cloth provides contrast of scale.
~ Lesley Riley

Here's another favorite photo. I use this one a lot
in my work. Feminine pinks in a variety of textures
(silk, organza, brocade) and bright happy prints
can work their own kind of magic. ~ Lesley Riley

Creativity is really the structuring of magic.
Anne Kent Rush

The greatest achievement was at first and for a time a dream. The oak sleeps in the acorn, the bird waits in the egg, and in the highest vision of the soul a waking angel stirs. Dreams are the seedlings of realities.
James Allen

SEEDLINGS

Using a photo from Darlene Troyer's "Soul in the Stone" image CD (http://www.magdalenamoon.com/), I enhanced the color saturation of the original image. The quote was in my quote stash and matched the image. ~ Lesley Riley

Above all, do not lose your desire to walk. I have walked myself into the best thoughts.
Soren Kierkegaard

Walked Myself

This is one of my favorite photos. I enhanced the hue in the black and white photo to give it a green cast suggestive of the outdoors. The orange background fabric and accompanying hues speak of fall.

~ Lesley Riley

fragment fabric bundle

RAINBOW

When I found this photo on eBay,
I went searching for just the right
quote to pair with it. I have many
quote books, and find a lot of them
in what I read, but it's always easiest
to type in a keyword on one of my
favorite online quote sites and find
just the right match! Doesn't that
blue squiggle background fabric
remind you of rain? ~ Lesley Riley

The way I see it, if you want the rainbow,
you gotta put up with the rain.
Dolly Parton

SHINE IT

I drew a Victorian-inspired color palette of fabrics from my stash to play up the time period of the photo – a rich brocade offset by a textured red. This girl's wistful look tells me that she is unsure of herself. The quote is a reminder to us all to be confident and true to ourselves.
~ Lesley Riley

Find your inner light and shine it on others.
Elizabeth Carey Lewis

Pay attention to what you do
so you can find out who you are.
Mary C Morrison

Who You Are

*This woman looks a little straight-laced and serious, but
sometimes that is a necessary part of accomplishing your
dreams. The color palette of the fabrics suggests order but
the punch of red adds a little excitement. Finding out who
you are can be exciting!~ Lesley Riley*

19

In every man's heart there
is anchored a little schooner.
Henry Miller

LITTLE SCHOONER

Blue fabrics were used to suggest water. Orange is the complement of blue and creates more interest in the piece along with the play of large and small patterns.
~ Lesley Riley

Fragments are fun and easy to make. Once you try creating a few and discover how marvelous they look, you'll get hooked! You'll want several for yourself and to give as gifts; any excuse to make more! They most definitely deserve to be on display and there are many ways to do so. Here are a few ideas:

FRAMES

On the preceding page we show you a fragment displayed in a distressed store-bought frame. You can alternately make your own frames from window panes, or use old vintage frames from flea markets or garage sales – any of these will bring character to the piece. Take them home and resize them to fit, or layer another piece of fabric behind if you desire. Don't forget to slip your fragments into a bag and bring them with you when you go frame shopping, as it sometimes seems a frame will just jump right out and speak to you for a particular fragment.

PILLOWS

Fragments look amazing on pillows. Sew them on and add pieces of matching fabric swatches here and there to tie into the color theme. Sew on vintage trims and buttons to embellish. (see page 82 and 83)

WALL HANGINGS

Fragments also stand on their own as a gift, given tissue-wrapped in a box. The receiver can enjoy it as is or hang on a wall. You can sew a 6" x 2" inch strip of fabric to the back to slip through a stained or painted wood dowel for hanging ease.

To me, there's a thin line between visual art and the art of the written word. In visual art, you tell stories with images. In writing, you create images with words. With Story Fragments, you combine the two to create personal, yet universal stories through image and word, using fabric as your vehicle.
- Lesley Riley

22

In addition to Lesley Riley's "Fragment Series", she does "Story Fragments" which look like small quilts. Here is what she has to say about how she initially came up with the idea of "Story Fragments".

"Originally, each Fragment I made came with a short story. I used the picture and the mood I had created with fabrics, as well as the quote, to inspire real or imagined ideas and put them into words. As the popularity of Fragments grew, I didn't have the time to write the stories and they fell by the wayside. Now I have found that the Fragment can do the story telling too.

I am a storyteller at heart. I find it fascinating the way different fabrics can suggest or tell a story - schoolgirl plaids, royal purple brocades. Taking the notion of fabric and story one step further, I wanted to create a "scene" from a story - an illustration - and give it depth and texture. Fabric can do this for me. Words are not always necessary, but I like the addition of text in my art.

You start by defining and refining your story – an outline, so to speak, to provide direction for the work. Then move on to your background; every story needs one. Yours could be a paint-dyed or printed cloth or combination. Use fabric to bring one or more characters to life, and create a setting or environment that completes your story fragment. Create artistic and/or realistic objects from fabric. Later on, your Story Fragments can be used to create books, quilts, whatever you envision as your story unfolds." ~ Lesley Riley

In the Garden
❧ Lesley Riley ❧

MATERIALS

FABRICS: Cottons; Silks; Vintage Rayons; Warm & Natural Cotton Batting by The Warm Company; Prepared Fabric by ColorTextiles

MARKERS/PENS: Micron Pigma Pen .05 Black by Sakura of America

OTHER: Pellon Wonder Under

TOOLS: Iron; Bernina Sewing Machine; Pins; Foam Brush

PRINTER: Epson C88 Printer with DURABrite Inks

INSTRUCTIONS

See Garden Party for Two - Page 28.

Garden Party for Two

❧ Lesley Riley ❧

MATERIALS

FABRICS: Cotton; Silks; #50 Pellon Interfacing or White Cotton or Muslin (for backing fabric; Pellon is stiffer than regular fabrics and adds more body to the piece but takes longer to dry); Vintage Rayon; Prepared Fabric by Color-Textiles

PAINTS: Fluid Acrylics Quinacridone Violet, Quinacrodine/Nickel Azo Gold, Quinacridone Magenta by Golden

MARKERS/PENS: Micron Pigma Pen .05 Black by Sakura of America

OTHER: Pellon Wonder Under; Painted Paper Towels for Leaves; Hannah Silk Ribbon; Yarn; Dyed Angora Hair

TOOLS: Iron; Bernina Sewing Machine; Pins

PRINTER: Epson C88 Printer with DURABrite Inks

INSTRUCTIONS

1. Cut Pellon to desired size and paint background piece with Golden fluid acrylics. Dry.

2. Print face and hands onto inkjet prepared fabric. Remove paper backing and back with Wonder Under before cutting out. Wonder Under prevents edges from fraying. Cut out.

3. Scale your figure so that the total length is about 7-8 times the length of the head including the head. (This is a classic rule for determining human figure proportions.). Rough-cut clothing and pin in place. Trust your eye to get the proportions correct.

4. To create dimension, add other objects (table, chair, tree) remembering that objects in the background should be smaller than those in the foreground. Cut some free-form and some true-to-life. Option: Ironing Wonder Under to back of fabrics before cutting gives them some stiffness and makes cutting easier. They can later be fused into place.

5. GARDEN PARTY FOR TWO ONLY - To create an accurate chair, look through home magazines or catalogs and find a chair shape that you like. Cut it out and enlarge it to fit into your Story Fragment. Print it in high contrast black and white onto copy paper. Lay a piece of Wonder Under slightly larger than the chair image over the copy (paper side up) and trace the outline of the chair. Iron Wonder Under onto the back of the fabric you have chosen for your chair. Cut out chair. This creates a REVERSE of the chair. If you prefer the exact orientation as seen in your photo, turn over your copy and trace from the back.

6. Iron to fuse face and hands into place.

7. Hand- or machine-sew clothing and other objects to background. Add additional decorative stitching and embellishment as desired, such as beading, ribbon embroidery, etc.

8. Write text onto background with Pigma pen.

I can enhance my mood and get inspired for story telling by the music I listen to or the movies I watch. Period costume movies are a great inspiration, along with a little Mozart. They can transport me to that time and place and I instinctively reach for fabrics and colors to complement the mood. Other times I work in silence with only the sunshine and the colors and textures in my fabric stash to inspire me. ~ Leslie Riley

Her Beauty Story Fragment

❧ Kristen Robinson ❧   *Student of Lesley Riley*

Lesley Riley teaches and facilitates mixed-media classes internationally, including how-to create a "Story Fragment". The next several pages are filled with artwork inspired by Lesley and created by those she mentored in the classroom.

HOW-TO CREATE A STORY FRAGMENT STEP-BY-STEP

MATERIALS

FABRICS: Cotton; Silk Shantung; Silk; Pellon Wonder Under; Burlap; EQ Printables by Electric Quilt; Satin, Lace and Other Scraps

FABRIC DYES: Tea (Chai, specifically)

MARKERS/PENS: Micron Pigma Pen .08 Dark Brown by Sakura of America

RUBBER STAMPS: Catherine's Secret, Arms and Legs and Crinoline de Can by Character Constructions

ADHESIVES: SoBo Fabric Glue by Delta

OTHER: Ribbons; Fibers; Yellow and Taupe Thread; Victorian Woman Image; Feathers; Photograph of Face (sized and printed on fabric)

TOOLS: Needle

PRINTER: Epson CX5000 or C88 with DURABright Inks

INKPADS: Black

STEP ONE
(DYING YOUR PIECE OF COTTON)

1. Cut a piece of white cotton approximately 13" x 15". Carefully submerse fabric into tea that has cooled. I prefer a black tea as it gives a bit of variation in color.
2. Soak for 5 minutes; remove and roll into a ball, securing with rubber bands.
3. Again immerse fabric in tea and soak until you have achieved desired color.
4. Set aside to dry.

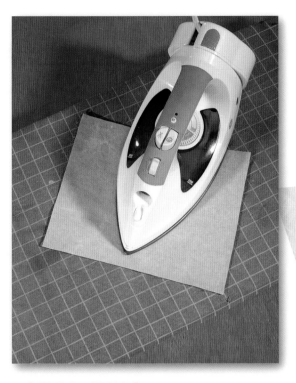

STEP THREE

1. After webbing has cooled, remove backing. Position burlap on the center of cotton background.

2. If you choose not to use webbing, apply burlap with appropriate fabric glue.

Note: it is extremely important that you set your piece aside until the glue has dried per the manufacturer's instructions, as the glue will seep through the fibers of the burlap when wet.

STEP TWO
(ADHERING THE BURLAP)

1. Cut out a rectangle from burlap that is approximately 6" x 4". Iron Wonder Under on the back.

STEP FOUR
(CREATING AND DRESSING YOUR FIGURE)

1. Cut a small piece of batting and sandwich between face printed on fabric and Wonder Under for demension. Iron in place and cut out face. Set aside to cool.

2. Stamp bodice, skirt, legs and arms onto back side of Wonder Under.

STEP FIVE
(CREATING THE BACKGROUND)

1. On adhered, cooled or sufficiently dried (if using glue) burlap, add two strips of silk shantung to either side, creating a billowing curtain effect. Tack down with hand-stitching or with fabric glue that is appropriate to use with silk.

2. Once curtains are in place, add a strip of gathered silky fabric at the top; this will create the valance for the curtains. Next, add a piece of clip art - printed onto either paper or fabric - to the center of burlap. Apply with a durable fabric-safe adhesive. Set aside to dry.

STEP SIX
(POSITIONING FIGURE ONTO BACKGROUND)

1. After you have cut out the garments, iron Wonder Under onto wrong side of cloth. Once webbing has cooled, remove from the back of the fabric and position onto background. Cut out and attach to create the figure's form.

2. To create the skirt, begin by layering strips of different fabric over the form. Apply enough pieces to create a full billowing look.

3. For the torso, begin wrapping a silky fabric to create fullness; you do not want this to be tight against the body.

4. After you have completed wrapping, add a strip of lace around the figure as you would a shawl.

5. Place face printed on fabric in position and iron in place.

STEP SEVEN
(ADDING YOUR FIGURE TO THE PIECE AND FINISHING TOUCHES)

1. In the center of the valance previously created, add a handful of bird feathers, making sure to sew them securely to the fabric.

2. Cut silk shantung or a similar fabric into 6 strips about 10" in length, then cut in half totaling 12 strips. Bring the 12 strips together and tie into a knot in the center. Pink the ends of strips at random lengths.

3. Place the center of strips over feathers, making sure to cover the stitching you used to attach them to the background. Next, sew or adhere strips to fabric piece.

4. To complete the composition, add journaling to your piece.

5. Finally, attach the piece to a sturdy piece of cardboard, gathering fabric in places to create a non-uniform look. Punch one hole on the left and another on the right, large enough to pass a strip of fabric through. Tie the strip off in back to ensure your piece is level when hanging on the wall.

At the time I created this piece I was reading about actresses in 18th century Europe. It occurred to me how many of us do not stop to think of the complete change that has occurred in the last 300 years in terms of the way we view women of the stage. During the 18th century, many women of the theatre were viewed as promiscuous (even though it was often not the case), actresses were in limbo between the upper and middle classes and the lower class of the time period.

This piece is my interpretation of the 18th century actress whose beauty and grace were admired by many, while under layers of lovely fabric her heart perhaps ached a little for that in which she would never have; respect, and for many, true love. I purposely left the edges of all the fabric frayed to reflect the unraveling that 18th century actresses experienced once their beauty began to fade and their admirers left town at the end of each season. I chose a face of a woman that reflects contemplation and perhaps a bit of recognition as to what lies on the path ahead. ~ Kristen Robinson

THE JOURNALING READS:
So full of light, her beauty her grace, each move,
each breath, glorious, unconscious delight. So this my
ode to the 18th century actress and a reminder of how
far all women have progressed.

She Was Told To Be Good

Deb Lewis · *Created in Lesley Riley's Class*

MATERIALS

FABRICS: White Cotton; Scraps of Plain and Printed Fabrics with Different Textures

PAINTS: Acrylic Paints by Golden

MARKERS/PENS: Black Permanent Marking Pen

ADHESIVES: Fabric Glue

OTHER: Yarn; Beads; Embroidery Floss; Thread; Ribbon; White Tags; Velvet Leaves; Photograph of Face (sized and printed on fabric)

TOOLS: Scissors; Pinking Shears; Needle

INSTRUCTIONS

1. Rough-sketch outline of design on scrap paper.
2. Completely dampen 12" x 15" piece of white cotton fabric with water and then paint as desired with acrylic paints. Iron dry to set paint.
3. Using the sketch as a guide, cut out desired shapes from various fabrics. Glue shapes onto painted and ironed background fabric. Adhere velvet leaves.
4. Using embroidery floss, sew a decorative stitch around selected elements of the design. Add desired beading.
5. Paint white tags and add wording with permanent marker pen.
6. Sew tags onto tree and bottom edging.
7. Add decorative ribbon pieces to bottom edge, cuffs and top of hat.

The inspiration for this fabric collage came from an original short story I had written about a young girl who dreamed of flying, but was always told by her mother to "be good" and be happy with the life that she had. The journaling on the tree tags read, "and so she lived her life with both feet planted firmly on the ground". The tags on the bottom are the thoughts that she aspires to: fly, dream, create, love, grow, believe, truth, beauty. ~ Deb Lewis

I created this piece with the utmost idea of honoring the things I truly love. I am enthralled with billowing fabrics, fibers and fluid motion in artwork. The thoughtful expression of this woman draws me into a realm where romance and the innocence of longing interlock. ~ Kristen Robinson

Her Hearts Desire

❧ Kristen Robinson ❧

For me this piece is about passion. Passion for all things that create a longing in us whether they are the love we feel for another or perhaps the passion that stirs when we create art, or something as simple as passion for a new day. ~ Kristen Robinson

MATERIALS

FABRICS: White Cotton; Silk Shantung; Silk; Ticking; EQ Printables by Electric Quilt; Pellon Wonder Under;

FABRIC DYES: Chromium Oxide Green, Red Oxide, Copper and Cerulean Blue Deep by Golden

MARKERS/PENS: Micron Pigma Pen .08 Dark Brown by Sakura of America

ADHESIVES: Fabric Glue

OTHER: Ribbons; Fibers; Beads; Yellow and Taupe Thread; Victorian Woman Image; Hat Pin; Flower Petal

TOOLS: Needle

PRINTER: Epson CX5000 or C88 with DURABright Inks

INSTRUCTIONS

1. Start with a piece of white cotton approximately 16" x 20". Use fluid acrylics to dye the fabric to resemble a landscape background; set aside to dry. Iron flat.

2. Dye a 6" x 30" strip of cotton with greens and browns. This will later be used for the hedges. Dry. Iron flat.

3. Choose or draw an appropriate head (approximately 2" high) for the body and print onto fabric. Before cutting out head, iron Wonder Under onto wrong side of cloth to prevent fraying. Once webbing has cooled, remove from back of fabric and position onto background. Iron to secure.

4. Draw or trace the figure's underskirt and bodice onto the back side of Wonder Under.

5. Once you have drawn garments, iron Wonder Under onto the wrong side of the cloth. Once webbing has cooled, remove from back of fabric and position onto background.

6. Use Wonder Under and draw an arch and a column for the garden way. Follow the above steps and position archway as desired onto background.

7. Once all elements are laid out, iron them onto background fabric.

8. Place additional fabric over underskirt to create a billowing look. Hand-sew the overskirt onto the piece.

9. Once figure and archway are properly attached, tear green and brown dyed cotton piece into ¼" strips, and cut them into 12" pieces. Accordian-fold each piece and tack down with fabric glue until you have a hedge effect.

10. Sew hedging to background using very small stitches. Randomly place an iridescent bead over stitches as you sew.

11. Use a fabric scrap to create a hat. Add strips of ribbon, a flower petal and hair pin.

12. Randomly sew knots of ribbon onto column of archway. Add green and brown fibers at the top of archway to represent foliage.

13. Create a ribbon rose and attach streamers to it; sew onto the resting place between the figure's hands.

14. Add journaling at the bottom of the fabric as desired.

I penned my inspiration before I started the quilt. This helped me determine how I wanted to construct my collage. I used my personal experiences to help guide my writing. ~ Amy Hahn

34

Transformation
❧ Amy Hahn ❧

MATERIALS

FABRICS: Lightweight White Cotton; Silks; Polyester Painted with Fabric Textiles; Upholstery Fabrics and Cotton Printed with Imagery from Music Scores; Birthday Card; Colorfast Sew-In Ink Jet Fabric Sheets by June Tailor; Cotton Batting; Wonder Under by Pellon

PAINTS: Quinacridone Violet, Phthalo Blue, Green Gold, Iridescent Bright Gold Fluid Acrylics and others by Golden

MARKERS/PENS: PITT Artist Pens by Faber-Castell

PASTELS/CHALKS: Green and White Portfolio Series Oil Pastels

OTHER: Velvet Leaves; Metal Charms by Blue Moon Glass; Glass Beads; Buttons; Threads; Coordinating Embroidery Thread; Ribbon; Faux Flowers

TOOLS: Scissors; Needles; Pliers (sometimes used to pull the needle through the many layers of fabric); HuskyStar 219 Sewing Machine by Husqvarna Viking (I like the simplicity of it and the fact that it sews through multiple layers easily)

PRINTER: HP Deskjet 940C

INSTRUCTIONS

1. Cut fabric for base to desired size.

2. Soak fabric prior to painting to help colors blend easily. Once soaked, paint background fabric with fluid acrylic wash as desired. Apply oil pastels on top of the paint to soften the edges. Allow fabric to dry.

3. Decide on images for collage by initially sketching on drawing pad.

4. Select fabrics to be used in collage. Iron on Wonder Under to back of the fabrics before cutting to keep from fraying and to help them adhere to base.

5. Next, cut out shapes in the various fabrics creating imagery desired. Remove backing from fabric and iron onto background fabric.

6. Add hand-stitching and embellishments.

7. Write story fragment on the quilt to create a "Story Quilt" or "Journal Quilt".

8. Create a frame for the journal quilt by sewing together selected fabric with batting on the inside.

9. Hand-sew finished fabric piece to binding to reinforce using a running stitch.

10. Add sleeve to the back of the quilt for hanging.

I created this quilt in a class taught by Lesley Riley called Story Fragments. I took the class because I have always wanted to add words to my art quilts and thought this would be a challenge. My favorite part is creating the collage… auditioning fabrics, selecting colors, cutting out shapes, watching it become a meaningful image; I feel that is the power behind my art. My inspiration came from a personal struggle with medical issues this last year as well as my work providing art therapy to children who have experienced trauma.

~ Amy Hahn

CHAPTER 8 $\mathcal{KC}$ Willis

"When I began to do fiber art, it was the Cowgirl who came riding into the forefront of my imagination. I'm surrounded in my studio by the faces of Annie Oakley, Sadie Austin and Pearl Heart. In my art the bond now grows stronger than ever. They were tough, strong, beautiful and brave. They were the Women of the West. They are my heroes."

KC Willis is a cowgirl at heart. Always was. Even though she grew up in Wisconsin, she was surrounded by her father's love of the Old West, listening to country music, watching TV westerns and dreaming about life on The Ponderosa. She eventually traveled west to the home in her heart, became a country western singer, published a novel with a sharp-shootin' cowgirl hero, and now is communicating with legendary femmes through her artwork, which she calls "mixed media cowgirl collage with attitude."

Her distinctive pieces sport sassy, feminist quotes, such as, "Pa said I could have my choice of any man; rather have my choice of any horse" and "I can shoot as good as any man… and look better doin' it". All KC's words are inspired by the women she so admires.

"I learned how to listen," she explains. "Maybe from being a singer I was all about listening. I looked at pictures of these incredible women and when I quieted the clatter in my head, they spoke every single time. Calamity Jane catches me so off guard sometimes that I laugh out loud at some of the things she says. My dogs look at me like I'm crazy."

Her dogs, Josie the chocolate Lab ("the happiest blind dog you'll ever see") and Fiona, a Corgie mix ("a pound hound, low to the ground") are an integral part of her family, one that she calls "The Waltons with iPods." They live in the foothills near Boulder, Colorado, where she met and last year married her husband, Logan. Ten years her junior, he has two sons, ages 12 and 14, and KC instantly became a step-mom.

"Never having had kids before, this is has been a big change for me. I've learned a lot – like my house doesn't have to perfect. Priorities shift. We like to throw the football; I throw a pretty mean spiral! We're very hokey; we like to play board games, we love to camp and to watch movies together. One of our favorite things to do is walk the blind dog to the park. We go to all my stepsons' sports: football, track and basketball. The 12-year-old paints and makes collages in my studio. In fourth grade he wrote that he wants to be an artist because "KC taught him how to be an artist."

KC turned her attention from painting to collage about six years ago and founded her business, Lipstick Ranch. The name, she says, just "…landed in my head. Great ideas can land in your head, but you have to be prepared to recognize them. If you don't expect magic or miracles or blessings, you won't see them when they are right in front of you. Sharpen your recognition skills because really good stuff happens all the time. You need to be able to say, I'll take that!"

It's this philosophy that, in part, has led Lipstick Ranch to its success. The studio, separate from the house, is a bevy of activity. "I ship pieces out so fast, I almost don't remember making them!" KC describes a typical day as hectic, with she and her assistants "standing on our heads" to meet each deadline.

"The studio looks just like what we do in there – it's improv - it's about grabbing notes out of the air. It's stuffed with bowls and bowls of buttons and rhinestones, enough fabric to cover Pike's Peak, three or four work tables and a couple of Sears sewing machines; they're work horses and are as simple as the lives of the women in my art." Like KC's heroes, she also brandishes a smoking gun; a paint-stripping heat gun that burns the edges of the papers and fabrics, making them look older still.

KC also produces a line of western-themed greeting cards for Leanin' Tree, and along with her husband, collects and revitalizes vintage furniture, which she sells to local stores and interior designers. Her website, www. lipstickranch.com offers everything from wall hangings and pillows to slip covers and clothing.

"I've always felt I'm not some brilliant person. Do I take advantage of opportunities that come my way? Yeah, I do. But these are gifts from God – He keeps giving me these creative gifts and I take them for a ride."

My work is about extremes – it looks old, it sounds new – it's got great female and male energy; it's got rust and rhinestones. Life is about extremes, this world certainly is today. I think that's why women respond so well to my work. The familiarity of the old fabrics, the old quilts, maybe your grandmother's … but also recognition of the strength that you have inside yourself."

KC finds many of her wonderful fabrics and embellishments - lace, fringe, doilies, swatches of embroidered tablecloths - on eBay. The vintage images come from history books, old postcard collections and photos that people send.

From time to time, KC uses at-risk youth to help her with her prep work, such as coffee-staining yards of fabric in huge restaurant stockpots and draping it over a fence to dry. ("It looks like The Real McCoys moved in and hung out their laundry.")

This frees the artist to make her special brand of magic, which includes mentoring teenagers. "These kids take pride in their work; they see that art can be a business, and that they can be a part of it." KC is working on a degree in art therapy and counseling and also conducts workshops at a residential center for troubled girls in Denver. She admits to having made mistakes in her own life and battling bipolar disorder. Her goal is to help turn young lives around.

"Collage is taking bits that, in and of themselves, might seem ugly and worthless, rearranging them and they become works of art. It's same with these girls. I teach them there are no 'throw away' people. I'm passionate about being alive. And about second chances. Through my art I give old fabrics, buttons and lace a second chance, and I give these women from our past a second chance to say something new. And in turn they give me a second chance to do something right."

KC Willis on Collage
(STEP-BY-STEP)

Each fabric collage piece starts with unprimed, light-weight artist canvas that has been torn to size, washed and coffee-dyed. I rarely, if ever, actually cut fabric. The tearing and then washing of the canvas will fray the edges of the fabric and leave plenty of tangled threads in the bottom of the washer. These will come in handy later; set them aside to dry.

The coffee-staining is done pretty much the way pioneer women probably washed their clothes. Huge stock pots are put on the stove. The water is warmed enough for the instant coffee (whatever brand is buy-one-get-one-free that week) to dissolve. The fabric is dipped (not soaked) until saturated, immediately tossed, dripping wet, into a bucket and carried outside where it is literally thrown over a fence in the backyard of my studio. Sometimes there is a line of fabric a half-acre long. I learned the hard way not to fill up the fence on days when the wind might kick up. It is a rare piece of fabric that does not find itself dipped in coffee and thrown on my fence.

The canvas then has a piece of fabric placed onto the back of it and sewn around the edges, just inside the frayed edges. There is no middle layer of fabric or batting. The layers will be added to the outside of the piece, not the inside. Before I begin to add the layers of collaged fabrics to the canvas, I burn the frayed edges. The fray turns a deep brown, which complements the aged look of the work and adds its own "frame." I do many pieces a week and have found lots of ways to do things as quickly as possible. When it comes to burning… I don't mess around. No crafter's gun for me. I use the high heat of a paint-stripping gun... singed fabric or corregated cardstock in the blink of an eye!

Typically, I start with a layer of old pillow ticking fabric and then add layers of old and new fabrics, in smaller pieces, on top of that. My work is very much about texture. Cut velvets and thick brocades intermingled with calicoes. I love old fabrics with holes in them. The holes let you peek through to the layer beneath, just like the women in the photos I use let you peek through to the past.

I don't use pins… I have a blind dog that likes to lie under my work-table and, besides her safety, it's too time consuming. I often lay out a dozen pieces at a time. So I simply apply a very light bit of Tacky Glue to the backs of the fabrics and set them aside. While they are drying I work on the other dozen or so pieces that are always underway. Once dried, I sew around the edges of the fabric using a variety of stitches. My sewing machine of choice is a very inexpensive (less than $500) Sears Kenmore Computerized Sewing Machine. It's all I have ever used. They are true work-horses. (I think it's what Calamity would have used.)

MATERIALS:

FABRICS: Canvas, Floral Patterned Cotton; Seude (not all fabric shown in this photo), Corrugated Cardboard; Fringe; Ribbon; Canvas; Junk Jewelry; Vintage or Fancy Butttons.

OTHER: coordinating Fabric for the back; Instant Coffee

STEPS TO CREATE KC WILLIS FABRIC WALLHANGINGS

STEP ONE

1. Wash canvas in warm water and dry.
2. Pull threads of edges to create a fringe border.
3. Next coffee-dye all canvas, fabrics, lace and trims.

STEP TWO

1. Sew coffee-dyed canvas to a piece of coordinating patterned fabric to create a front and a heavy foundation to continue the wall hanging.

STEP THREE

1. The fabric collage wall hanging is now thee layers. The front is shown in the photograph.
2. Flip fabric layers over. Sew on suede.

STEP FOUR

1. Continue to sew lace and trims to the front of the fabric collage.

1. The photo transfers start with the image scanned into my computer and printed up on photo-transfer paper. The image is then applied to coffee-stained canvas using heat.

2. Tear corrugated cardboard the size of the image transfer. CAREFULLY burn edges with a heat gun outside in well-ventilated area.

3. Sew transfer onto singed cardboard.

On days when I'm not actually putting pieces together, my assistant and I will get the photo transfers together. I find, because we do so many pieces a month, the best way is to spend entire days doing one aspect of the work or another. One day I'll tear and wash fabric, coffee-stain and place it on my fabric shelves. Another day, we might do 50 photo transfers and a pile of mini-collages that we will later use to embellish the piece.

Once we have sewn down the fabric layers that make up the main fabric collage, we will glue down the photo transfer that will be the heart of the piece. Before I even start a piece, I know which western woman will go onto it. Her personality will dictate the fabric colors and choices. My need to satisfy my texture-fix will be the other factor in fabric selection.

The photo transfers start with the image scanned into my computer and printed up on photo-transfer paper. The image is then applied to coffee-stained canvas using heat. A piece of torn, corrugated cardboard or other textured, thick paper is torn slightly larger than the image itself, and the edges that show are burned using the same heat gun. Since where there is smoke there is fire, pieces are always carefully checked before they are brought back into the studio. If we are going to leave the studio shortly after one of our infamous pyro sessions, all singed items are left outdoors… just in case. The image is glued down to the burnt paper and later the edges are sewn (yes, the cardboard is run through the sewing machine). Here is where the work-horse factor of the Sears Kenmore comes in handy.

Once the photo transfer on cardboard is glued down to the center of the piece, an appropriate quote needs to accompany the image. Through the years I have written probably close to 100 quotes. Some of them are flexible and can roam from piece to piece, some are written with one girl in mind and will always be her words. The first few pieces I made didn't have quotes on them. It didn't take long, though, for the girls to start talking to me and I had no choice but to listen. The quotes are written on a heavyweight, unprimed artist canvas that has also been coffee-stained. I write them by hand (they are not transferred) using a fine-point Sharpie. Sometimes burnt-edged paper is put behind the quote, sometimes it isn't. The edges of the quote are either sewn around or singed.

Now comes the fun part... when an artist's individual fairy dust is applied in the form of embellishments.

"Never did wanna play with dolls."

Lotta, knew a lady shouldn't flaunt her whip, but then Lotta was no lady."

LOTTA

I became aware at some point that fairies were really hot items. Everywhere I turned there were fairies on cards, fairies for your garden, fairies for gifts, etc. One day I asked myself how I could make fairies my own. Was there a way to do a Lipstick Ranch fairy? The phrase, "Outlaw Fairies" came to mind immediately! So I simply chose a few girls who I thought should have wings. Lotta Crabtree, being the lady she was, had just the right attitude to be an Outlaw Fairy. One with wings and a cigar! She spoke to me right away.

~ KC Willis

LULU

I wanted to celebrate the guts and sassiness of a woman who knew how to shoot and knew she looked good doing it. Rodeo star Lulu Parr has always been one of my favorite images. Every cowgirl should look so good! I chose fairly feminine fabrics, because Lulu was a lady if nothing else. The embellishments are also feminine and even a little glitzy. In the quote, though, we see how tough and cool she was.
~ KC Willis

Board Members

Can't forget the guys now can I? I do very few cowboys, but these two (several collectors have said these are the James Brothers) are among my favorites. This is a great sepia photograph showing them both dapper and dangerous. It's always a challenge for me to step away from "my girls" and have to choose fabrics and embellishments that honor the men of the west. So on this piece, I chose dark fabrics and silver embellishments that were tarnished. Bits of rust round out the perfect details for these two troublemakers. ~ KC Willis

"We growed up regular. Our Mama Taught us right. Reckon we just get bored..." Jesse

ANNIE'S 'TUDE

This hand-colored image of Annie Oakley is always fun to do. It adds quite a bit of color and pizzazz to pieces that typically don't have color in the photograph. Annie was one of the first women to be a true western hero to men and women alike and I love doing work that honors her spirit. Again, the fabrics are feminine and the details are sparkly to the extreme... just like Annie's skill and personality. Even though she reigned supreme in the world of male sharp-shooting, she was never anything but female. The quote I wrote for her lets us know that she was completely aware of the world she lived in, but she never let it stop her. ~ KC Willis

Designer Pillows ❧ KC Willis ❧

MATERIALS

FABRICS: Coffee-Dyed Canvas; Upholstery Fabric

OTHER: Photo; Photo Transfer Fabric; 17" x12" Pillow Form; Buttons; Thread; Pins

TOOLS: Sewing Machine; Pencil

INSTRUCTIONS

1. Cut two 18" x 12" template pieces of fabric.

2. Hem each piece inside edge 1". There will now be two pieces for the back.

3. Layer the hemmed edges over one another to get an 18"x 18" piece for pillow back; pin layered outside edges together. This layering will create an opening to insert pillow once sides are all sewn. MAKE CERTAIN YOU DO NOT SEW OPENING SHUT.

FRONT:

1. Cut one 18" x 18" piece of fabric.

2. Design, collage and layer a selection of desired small fabric swatches onto piece.

3. Follow manufacturer's instructions and transfer photo.

4. Add photo transfer image to front as shown with fancy sewing stitch.

5. Write saying on a cut, frayed and coffee-dyed canvas. Sew to pillow.

6. Add buttons if desired.

SEW PILLOW:

1. Place back and front pieces of prepared pillow fabric together, inside out.

2. Take out pins from back and re-pin back to front for sewing.

3. Sew together and lift foot, changing the stitch direction at all four corners to make a right angle at each. Complete a square all the way around.

4. Once finished, diagonally trim excess fabric with scissors at a 45 degree angle on all of the pillow's corners to allow shape once turned inside out. Open seams and press outward.

5. Turn pillow inside out. Push out corner angles with eraser tip to shape.

7. Slip in pillow form. Place in a special spot in your home to see and enjoy daily.

"I painted my own reality"

From time to time I like to step away from my cowgirls (believe it or not) and when I do, I always turn to the beauty of Native American women or the brightness of Frieda Kahlo.

I chose to do these women in pillows, because pillows are a great way to bring them close. They are right there on the sofa with you!
~KC Willis

My Love

❧ Lisa Engelbrecht ☙

MATERIALS

FABRICS: Canvas and Various Fabrics

FABRIC DYES: Adirondack Dye Sprays by Ranger

PAINTS: Blue-Green Acrylic; Lumiere Halo Blue-Gold by Jacquard Products

MARKERS/PENS: Brause Dip Pens; Purple Disappearing Ink Fabric Pen

RUBBER STAMPS: Local Craft Store

INKPADS: Blue FW Acrylic Ink by Daler-Rowney

ADHESIVES: Yes! Paste by Ganes Brothers & Lane

OTHER: Alphabet Stencils; Ribbon; Charms

TOOLS: Paintbrush; Scissors; Sprayer; Singer Sewing Machine

INSTRUCTIONS

1. Use an old paintbrush to make a square of color with blue-green acrylic and Halo blue-gold paints.

2. Use a sprayer on the Halo to bring out the underlying color.

3. On another piece of canvas, use tag board alphabet letters and Ranger dye sprays to stencil the word "love". Cut out and sew to larger background piece.

4. Cut squares of fabric and dried washes in various sizes and arrange on larger wash; sew on.

5. Write a quote using Brause pen and blue FW acrylic ink. You can lay this out first with a purple disappearing fabric pen.

6. Layer fabric, ribbon, trim and ephemera; sew on or adhere with Yes! Paste.

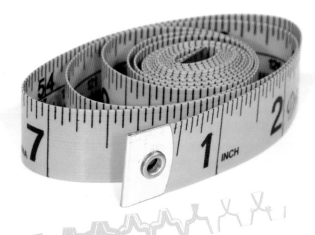

This is a spontaneous quilt that has developed over a couple of months... I'll put it away and then take it out and work on it... I think it's about done! It's hard to know when to stop before creating too much clutter. Decide on a main focal point; someplace for your eye to rest. Also be sure to leave corresponding white space for every mark you make or fabric you layer.
~ Lisa Engelbrecht

This piece came about like all my others - unplanned and spontaneous. I loved this gift wrap and tried to pick up the light turquoise color in the background. I just start layering and casting about for things that would fit and they seemed to jump onto the page – though there are always some adjustments. I was about to put away my 2006 planner, which was the Four Agreements by Don Miguel Ruiz, and found some amazing texts in there. I always want to write out words that are meaningful to me. Sometimes I write my current emotions - sometimes the right quote will suddenly appear as this one did! ~ Lisa Engelbrecht

Share Love

❧ Lisa Engelbrecht ❧

MATERIALS

FABRICS: Unprimed Canvas; Fabric Scraps

PAPERS: Gift Wrap (for background)

PAINTS: Brown, Turquoise and White Acrylics; Gesso

MARKERS/PENS: Brause Dip Pens; Purple Disappearing Ink Fabric Pen

INKPADS: Brown FW Acrylic Ink by Daler-Rowney

ADHESIVES: Aleene's Jewel-It by Duncan Enterprises; Duo Adhesive by USArtQuest

OTHER: Heart Beads; Vintage Postage Stamp; Ribbon; Stick-On Letters; Charms; Hot Foil Pen Silver Foil Refills by Staedtler

TOOLS: Hot Foil Pen by Staedtler; Paintbrush; Scissors; Singer Sewing Machine (it's inexpensive and does straight and zigzag stitch)

INSTRUCTIONS

1. Use an old paintbrush to make a square of color using gesso, turquoise and brown acrylic.

2. Cut a square of gift wrap to fit into the square of color; sew on.

3. Write around the square with Brause pen in brown FW acrylic ink. You can lay this out first with a purple disappearing ink fabric pen.

4. On a small rectangle of fabric write the word "love" with Duo Adhesive; foil with silver by rubbing with a smooth-surfaced item, like a spoon. Or use a foil pen; just depress the button on the foil pen and it heats up. Once hot, start writing on the foil (shiny side up), and it will transfer to your fabric. (See page 61 for step-by-step of "Collage Foil Embellishment Technique".)

5. Layer fabric, ribbon and ephemera; sew on or adhere with Yes! Paste. Add heart beads with Aleene's Jewel-It.

6. Layer with pencil strokes in a frame.

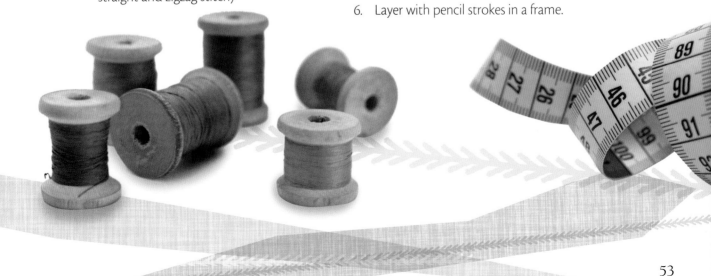

Love is the Star
❧ Lisa Engelbrecht ❧

MATERIALS

FABRICS: Various

PAINTS: Rust, Olive Green and Brown Acrylics

MARKERS/PENS: Brause Dip Pens; Hot Pen; Purple Disappearing Ink Fabric Pen

INKPADS: Rust, Green and Brown FW Acrylic Inks by Daler-Rowney

ADHESIVES: Duo Adhesive by USArtQuest

OTHER: Stick-On Letters; Charms; Hot Foil Pen Foil Refills by Staedtler in Gold

TOOLS: Hot Foil Pen by Staedtler; Paintbrush; Scissors; Singer Sewing Machine

INSTRUCTIONS

1. Use an old paintbrush to make a square of color in rust, olive green and brown acrylic paints.

2. Cut squares of fabric to fit into the square of color; sew on.

3. Write around the square with Brause pen in brown, rust and green FW acrylic ink. You can lay this out first with a purple disappearing ink fabric pen (available at fabric stores).

4. Layer fabric heart, ribbon and ephemera; sew on or adhere with Yes! Paste.

5. .Foil around heart by using a paint brush and outlining it with Duo Adhesive; allow adhesive to dry. Foil-emboss by rubbing foil onto dried adhesive with a smooth-surfaced item, like a spoon. Or use a foil pen; just depress the button on the foil pen and it heats up. Once hot, start writing on the foil (shiny side up), and it will transfer to your fabric. (See page 61 for step-by-step of "Collage Foil Embellishment Technique".

I found this heart at a fabric store. It fit perfectly with my "love" quotes. I like doing a gothic style of writing around the square - and just dipped in a couple colors of ink while I was writing to get a variegated effect. On the background of the heart I used some paste paper fabric that I absolutely love.
~ Lisa Engelbrecht

This started as a sample piece for my Spontaneous Quilt Class at the International Quilt Show. There are many techniques and washes that were integrated with fabric scraps. I sewed most of it and added some couched trim to unify the elements.
~ Lisa Engelbrecht

Wish

❧ Lisa Engelbrecht ❧

MATERIALS

FABRICS: Canvas and Various Fabrics

FABRIC DYES: Adirondack Dye Sprays by Ranger

MARKERS/PENS: Brause Dip Pens; Purple Disappearing Ink Fabric Pen

INKPADS: Pearlescent FW Acrylic Ink by Daler-Rowney

OTHER: Charms; Stencils

TOOLS: Paintbrush; Scissors; Singer Sewing Machine

INSTRUCTIONS

1. Use an old paintbrush to make a square of various colors.

2. Cut squares of fabric and arrange; sew on.

3. Write the word "wish" with Brause pen and Pearlescent ink. You can lay this out first with a purple disappearing ink fabric pen.

4. Layer fabrics, ribbon, trim and ephemera; sew on or adhere with Yes! Paste.

I have a thing for hearts! I saw a simple pillow at a store, copied the pattern and made some adjustments. This started a whole slew of hearts - using a lot of washes on canvas that were in my pile of unused washes - waiting to be pillows, I guess! I just developed a class on them as they are so easy to make and look great in various sizes hanging on the wall.
~ Lisa Engelbrecht

Heart

❧ Lisa Engelbrecht ❧

MATERIALS

FABRICS: Canvas; Cotton Batting or Cotton Balls (for stuffing); Various Fabrics; Felt

PAINTS: Gesso

MARKERS/PENS: Brause Dip Pens; Micron Pigma Pen by Sakura of America

INKPADS: Purple and Walnut FW Acrylic Inks by Daler-Rowney

ADHESIVES: Yes! Paste by Ganes Brothers & Lane

OTHER: Stick-On Letters; Charms; Wire; Gold Embossed BIrd; Coins or Ephemera

TOOLS: Paintbrush; Scissors; Singer Sewing Machine

INSTRUCTIONS

1. Cut two hearts out of canvas - they don't have to be perfectly symmetrical but should match somewhat.
2. Use an old paintbrush to make a wash of color with gesso, purple and walnut acrylic on the front side of the heart. Allow to dry.
3. Sew some lines as shown on front heart. Write "love always" with a Micron pen.
4. Cut squares of fabric to fit under the charms you choose; sew or glue onto front.
5. Layer fabric heart, ribbon and ephemera; sew on or adhere with Yes! Paste. Let dry overnight.
6. Sew the two pieces, decorated sides together, with a ½" seam, leaving a small opening on one side. Turn inside out.
7. Cut the edge around pillow in a zigzag or scalloped pattern.
8. Stuff pillow with cotton balls or batting; sew heart closed.
10. Insert wire through the top of the right side of the heart, twist across the top and insert it into the other side. Twist securely.
11. Hang on your wall, doorknob or decorative hook.

This foil technique not only works on fabric, but also on paper, tiles and even rocks!
~ Lisa Engelbrecht

STRUE

Lisa Engelbrecht
Lettering, Multi Media, Classes
please visit my website!: www.lisaengelbrecht.com
New! My blog at www.lisaletters.blogspot.com

True & Gratitude
Collage Foil Embellishment Technique

both by Lisa Engelbrecht

MATERIALS

FABRICS: Fabric of Choice

MARKERS/PENS: Hot Foil Pen by Staedtler; Purple Disappearing Ink Fabric Pen

ADHESIVES: Duo Embellishing Adhesive by USArtQuest

OTHER: Hot Foil Pen Refill in Gold Foil by Staedtler; Calligraphy Paper Script Sample from John Neal Bookseller

TOOLS: Inexpensive Paintbrush; Hot Foil Pen by Staedtler

INSTRUCTIONS

1. Create a Calligraphy Collage (basic instructions on previous pages). Allow room to add a foil letter or foil name.

2. Step-by-Step of Foil Embellishment Process: Pour a bit of Duo Embellishing Adhesive into a small cup. Outline your initial from the calligraphy paper script sample on the fabric (or paper) using a purple disappearing ink pen.

3. Next, use a small, inexpensive brush to outline the letter with Duo. After you've outlined the letter, flood it entirely with Duo, creating an even texture. Be sure to wash your brush out completely.

4. Let glue dry overnight.

5. Place a sheet of foil, shiny side up, on top of the glued initial. Rub firmly with a hot foil pen, making sure to apply pressure to the sides of the initial.

6. Carefully pull the foil back and voila! You'll have instant gold! Keep any bits of leftover foil for use in another project – don't throw them away!

The framed "Gratitude" collage was a thank you gift to Jill; to personalize it I foiled her name and initial.
~ Lisa Engelbrecht

Enjoy the Magic!
Julie McCullough

CHAPTER 10

JULIE Mc CULLOUGH

"We get hesitant as we grow older. We're so afraid to try new things for fear we will do them 'wrong'. Kids don't do that - they jump right in. I learned a lot about teaching adults from teaching children. As women, we are taught there's a right way and a wrong way, and you have to get past that!"

Don't give Julie McCullough a script, a recipe or a set of rules. She does things her way, whether it's speaking to a crowd, cooking a meal or creating the fairies for which she has become famous. Her dolls and wall hangings are exhibited in galleries across the country; she has been featured in nearly every doll making magazine on the market and in many books, including Patti Culea's "Creative Doll Making" and Susanna Orrayan's "Anatomy of the Doll" and "Finishing the Doll" among others. She was a guest on The Carol Duval Show on HGTV in a segment that continues to air, perpetuating even more interest and orders every time.

Though Julie has traveled extensively to teach, she now prefers to hold workshops at home in Iowa in her bright walk-out basement, a 1,000 square-foot studio she describes as incredibly colorful. "Every wall is a different color - purple, lime green, orange, checkered black and white," she says. "There are lots of antique cabinets with cubby holes I can stuff fabric in. I'm inspired by nature so I have lots of nature items around – rocks, bones, feathers – it's so unique. My students love it because I have everything here."

The rest of her home also reflects her free-spirited approach to art and life in general. Cathedral ceilings in her kitchen render the tops of her cabinets a veritable canvas of creativity, as she's used every inch of the eight feet of space. "There are a couple of chairs that belonged to my grandparents; a collection of Mexican pottery, some vintage toys and jars; part of an old banister; and a Valentines Day gift from my husband - four wooden wheels from a gypsy wagon, painted like circus wagon wheels. My house is a blend of items I treasure – it's eclectic and definitely not for everyone! My mother would want to know how you dust it. And I say… dust?"

While Julie and her husband spent most of their lives in Nebraska, his career in theatre necessitated moves to Pennsylvania and most recently to Iowa. Her new home has brought her old comforts as it backs up to a greenbelt. "I like woods, I love all the animals. Last night I looked outside and there was a fox walking by I just thought it was thrilling."

Though nature's influence is evident in her work, it's the theater that is her main inspiration, from shows like Cirque du Soleil to the Lion King. Her son, who also in the theater, and his new bride live in New York. Julie counts this as one of her favorite destinations not only for seeing a show, but also for finding fabulous fabrics.

"I love to shop in the Garment District – it's so inspirational. There are four or five blocks of stores that are nothing but fabrics, or buttons or trims that you absolutely never see anywhere else. It's sensory overload." She'll use cottons and more traditional, easy-to-find fabrics for her doll patterns and kits to ensure success, especially for beginners, but when she makes a doll to sell or exhibit at a gallery show, she can "go all out." In either case, each doll making day begins before she even gets out of bed.

"I lie in bed in the morning and mentally play with my pieces, and that's how I get a lot of work done. Some doll makers think of their dolls as their children and talk to them like they're people. To me, it's more like solving a math problem even though I don't do math. I have to think it through, step by step. It's trial and error, but most of the trial and error is in my head." Once in her studio, she answers e-mails, fills orders and cuts and sews during the day. Next, she takes a large box of

doll pieces upstairs to stuff. "That's when the cats begin to play; they chase doll heads around", she laughs. "They are very curious. One is on the work table all the time."

Julie was always artistic and majored in art in college. But she never imagined fabric would ultimately be her medium. Working with fabric involved sewing. And not being a rule follower, sewing, with its patterns and directions, held little appeal. She did enjoy macramé, crocheting and tie-dying (it was the 60's) which later led to weaving, dying and making cloth dragons for Renaissance festivals.

"I was a 'Dragon Lady' and eventually created wizards and other characters to go with the dragons. When I started doing dolls I looked through pattern books… the styles were Raggedy Anne and Cabbage Patch – and that's not what I had in mind! The best and worst thing that happened to me was I didn't know any other doll makers; there were no resources. This was before computers and I was working in a vacuum and now I'm so glad because I had to rely on my own creativity."

Julie is the only artist in a family of scientists, a fact that used to puzzle her father. "I explained that it's the same thought process. You have a set of givens, which for me is fabric and thread and stuffing, and then it's a lot of 'what ifs'. You start playing with the possibilities and that's what a scientist does. You've got certain things you can't change and you rearrange the things you can; that's what an artist does. To that he said proudly, 'Okay then, you get your artistic ability from me!'"

Julie's has many fond memories of her father, particularly of childhood camping trips and hikes through the forest. "He was sort of a free-spirit too, the typical absent-minded professor. He would take me on hikes in the woods and point out different types of mushrooms and lichens… and I would see fairies."

Today, those wonderful fairies live in the Enchanted Forest at www.magicthreads.com.

Mulberry Fairy

❧ Julie McCullough ❧

MATERIALS

FABRICS: Velour; Cotton; Lace; Handmade Fabric

PAINTS: Acrylics

OTHER: Yarn; Ribbon Roses; Cold Water Soluble Stabilizer; Dyed Wool; Ribbon; Angelina Fibers by Embellishment Village; Quilt Batting, Doll Kit by Julie at www.magicthreads.com

TOOLS: Glue Gun; Bernina Sewing Machine; Templates by Julie at www.magicthreads.com

STEP 1

Trace templates onto desired fabric for body parts and cut out.

STEP 2

Sew parts, turn inside out and stuff. Close hole by hand-sewing. Assemble doll's arms, legs and head to body.

STEP 3

Spray lace to dampen. Paint lace; allow to dry.

STEP 4

Gather lace and sew to doll's waist for skirt.

STEP 5

Sandwich dyed wool, ribbon, yarn and Angelina Fibers between layers of stabilizer.

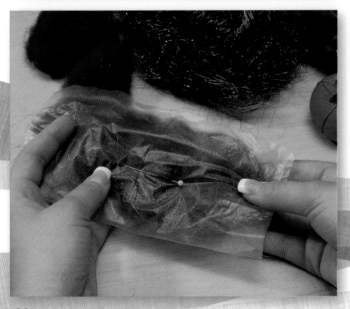

STEP 6

Cover with machine stitching.

STEP 7

Dip into water to "melt off" stabilizer.

STEP 8

Pull off all remaining stabilizer with fingers.

STEP 9

Cut a piece of the sewn fiber fabric for a small top for fairy; stitch to body.

STEP 10

Add a headband made from sewn fibers.

STEP 11

Make pom-pom wig from eyelash yarn; glue to head for hair. Insert eyes.

67

STEP 12

Make the wings out of cotton with a layer of quilt batting inside. Top-stitch a design onto the wings, then stitch wings onto the doll's back.

STEP 13

Accent with ribbon roses. Add eyebrows and lips with fine tip marker.

I like to name my Fairies after flowers and plants. Mulberry is one of those great words that evokes childhood memories of warm summer days. I remember picking plumb, juicy mulberries that stained your fingers and tongue with that delicious color. It's always been one of my favorites. ~ Julie McCullough

Imp

❦ Julie McCullough ❧

MATERIALS

FABRICS: Velour; Cotton; Lame; Pleated Silk

PAINTS: Metallics

MARKERS/PENS: Pigma Pens by Sakura of America

OTHER: : Hot Foil Pen Refill in Gold Foil by Staedtler; Calligraphy Paper Script Sample from John Neal Bookseller

TOOLS: Inexpensive Paintbrush; Hot Foil Pen by Staedtler

My Bernina sewing machine is over 25 years old and is a real work horse - nothing fancy, but nothing breaks either! ~ Julie McCullough

INSTRUCTIONS

1. Sew doll body and head with velour; stuff.

2. Needle-sculpt the face and draw on features with Pigma pens. Glue on animal eyes.

3. Use cotton fabric for doll legs; sew, stuff and joint together with small buttons.

4. Create arms in the same manner, but use velour for the bottom of the arms. Needle-sculpt hands.

5. For the doll's bodice, use an assortment of lace, dyed wool, Angelina fibers, ribbon and yarn sandwiched between layers of cold water soluble stabilizer. Stitch all over to anchor all the pieces together. When the piece is rinsed out the stabilizer dissolves and leaves the lace fabric. (See step-by-steps pages 64 - 69.)

6. Used pleated silk for skirt and dyed mohair for hair.

7. Make wings from lame fabric, stuffed and wired. Paint with metallics, allow to dry and sew onto the doll's back. Add wire antennae.

This Imp is just another interpretation of the Fairy form. I've done hundreds of fairies. I don't have inspirations as much as I see finished dolls in my head. The challenge is trying to create that vision in cloth.
~ Julie McCullough

71

Flower Girl

❧ Julie McCullough ❧

MATERIALS

FABRICS: Cotton

PAINTS: Acrylics; Metallics

MARKERS/PENS: Pigma Pens
by Sakura of America

OTHER: Braided and Floral
Upholstery Trims; Lace; Beads;
Petals; Ribbon Roses; Colored
Pencils; Plastic Eyes (6 mm)

TOOLS: Glue Gun; Bernina
Sewing Machine

INSTRUCTIONS

1. Sew doll using white cotton fabric. Stuff and assemble.

2. Paint on clothes, allow to dry.

3. Add pieces of heavy lace to arms and legs; embellish with beads and metallic paints. Let dry.

4. Use floral trim for skirt. Adorn shoulders with petals accented with ribbon roses.

5. Needle-sculpt face and glue in 6mm plastic eyes. Draw eyebrow and mouth with Pigma pens. Shade with colored pencils.

6. Unbraid upholstery trim and glue on for hair; accent with additional floral trim.

When I was a child we lived in the woods in Tennessee. I read lots of fairy tales and imagined I saw fairies everywhere. Many of my dolls are wood spirits and fairies. I get most of my inspiration from the woods around our house. A combination of flower colors will get me started on a new doll. This was one of those flashes!

Jack Flash

❧ Julie McCullough ❧

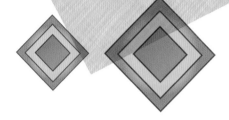

MATERIALS

FABRICS: Velour; Cotton; Velvet; Satin

PAINTS: Acrylics

MARKERS/PENS: Pigma Pens by Sakura of America

OTHER: Lace; Quilting; Beads; Sequins; Assorted Trims; Colored Pencils, Plastic Animal Eyes (6mm); Dowel; Box

TOOLS: Glue Gun; Bernina Sewing Machine

INSTRUCTIONS

1. Cover box with fabric. Decorate with stitching and sequins.

2. Create doll body from cotton, giving the doll a square bottom so it rests in the box.

3. Sew arms and hands; stuff. Insert hands into sleeve openings and hand-stitch in place. Add trim around the sleeves. Sew arms onto the sides of the doll.

4. Piece together headdress and stuff to form all the points of the jester cap. Needle-sculpt face and draw with Pigma pens and colored pencil. Accent with paint; allow to dry. Glue on animal eyes. Make pompoms and add to hat.

5. Place dowel in sleeve casing. Sew into body opening and neck.

6. Paint lace with acrylic paint and allow to dry. Gather painted lace around the neck. Top-stitch cotton for the second collar piece and add around neck.

The idea for Jack Flash came from a performance by Cirque du Soleil. I love their outrageous characters and costumes. This doll was originally designed as a challenge doll on Joggles website. It was constructed very basically in black and white and the challenge was for contestants to add the "bling". The winner was on the cover of Art Doll Quarterly. ~ Julie McCullough

If I had hands I'd caress the petals of the rose

If I had wings of black, I'd soar on the winds

Envy

❧ Julie McCullough ❧

MATERIALS

FABRICS: Canvas; Cotton

PAINTS: Acrylics; Metallics

OTHER: Wool Yarn; Ribbon; Angelina Fibers by Embellishment Village; Beads; Hot Water Soluble Stabilizer; Wooden Frame; Vintage Pillowcase Lace and Doilies; Polyester Batting

TOOLS: Heat Gun; Glue Gun; Bernina Sewing Machine

INSTRUCTIONS

1. Start with canvas and stitch a basic landscape using old lace and pillowcase edging to create rows of plants, hills, grasses and flowers.

2. Paint these with acrylic washes. Allow to dry.

3. For tree trunks, outline wool yarn with hot glue, cover with embossing powder and burnish. Use doilies for leaves.

4. Continue adding layers of paint until you are happy with the colors.

5. The woman and the crow are three-dimensional and made of cotton. Stuff them with polyester batting and add last.

I love woods, mossy old stone walls and crows, so this piece is simply about my favorite things. Many of the old lace and doilies I used were made by my grandmother and great grandmother. They had always sat unused in a box. I am now using them in my work, partly to give them a new use but also to show respect for the women in my family who created beautiful things with their hands. ~ Julie McCullough

CHAPTER 11

Jill Haglund

Jill Haglund, Founder, Owner and Creative Director of TweetyJill Publications (www.tweetyjill.com), sees herself first as an artist, and then as a publisher. Fascinated by photography, she began capturing memories on film as a young child and preserving them in imaginative, artful ways. As an adult, her love of creating art led her from teaching crafts to authoring books and running a successful publishing company. Yet, she always affords time to dabble at craft projects here and there, even with an incredibly busy production schedule.

Jill is no stranger to multitasking – besides creating her own style of collage artwork, teaching national and international classes and attending the most prestigious industry trade shows, she consistently produces several best-selling books at a time. With titles numbering near 18, her books are available at retail craft, fabric and book stores and at www.tweetyjill.com.

The now internationally-known company is one of very meager beginnings, and Jill's story proves that hard work and passion pay off. She had taught hundreds of classes for Creative Memories, spreading the joy of scrapbooking like wildfire and generating tremendous excitement. But in her travels she discovered a real need for quality "how-to" books, and left to launch a new dream.

Jill created her first book 11 years ago – making photocopies

in her closet and hand-binding each one. Within six months she had sold nearly 1,000 copies from multiple orders via e-mail and was shipping a car trunk load of books daily. The overwhelming response to her work led her to publish professionally, adding the work of other artists, editors and graphic designers.

As president of TweetyJill Publications, Jill was sought after for her humorous approach, nurturing spirit and inimitable talents to teach classes at Exposures in New York, The Retail Scrapbook Association Trade Shows, Craft & Hobby Industry Association Conventions, Barnes & Noble Booksellers and many retail scrapbook and stamp stores. As her company has grown exponentially, she continues to teach - as time permits - at various venues, with a five-day workshop on collage art scheduled for 2008 in Cortona, Italy (http://hometown. aol.com/infotuscany/MeetJillHaglund.html). But whether or not she is not teaching, she's always encouraging and inspiring everyone from the novice to the seasoned crafter with her cutting-edge books.

Jill covets her creative life and her "cozy" studio - where she can see something to work on in every corner. "I love looking around and seeing a rainbow of paint colors in an antique wire basket; paintbrushes in small vintage milk bottles; jars filled with old buttons; trunks of ephemera and vintage pictures;

basket upon basket full of fabric, trims and lace just waiting to be pulled to the sewing machine. My studio is a fun, 1,200 square foot space overlooking the studio of the photographer I work with. What a great open view!"

Her studio is a delightful melange of eclectic secondhand and antique furniture: hutches, cabinets, desks, chests and dressers. In the center is an oversized wooden work table that is always filled with art materials and the latest art projects. "Being a publisher has many benefits - one fabulous perk is being required to have on hand at all times the latest products available to work with. Now that is heaven for all artists!"

She even has a Guest Desk for visitors. Walk in, sign the guest book and then sit with Jill to create a "unique little something" of your own to take home.

Of her studio, specials gifts, burgeoning business and life in general, she admits, "Sometimes it seems like a dream - I often feel the need to pinch myself! I am very careful not to take this all for granted. I credit the Lord for my health, creativity and abundance of support I get from family, friends and co-workers."

Her three college-aged children, Lindsay, Matthew and Jason, are the nucleus of her support network and often the inspiration for art. "Times today, memories of yesterday and pictures of them throughout their lives are part of what keeps the energy going at full force at TweetyJill Publications," she explains.

Jill's favorite personal artwork involves creating collages using paper or fabric with vintage script, old text pages, music and photos, bird and nature images, postage stamps and ephemera. She scans a lot of images and prints them onto printable fabric - creating a transfer to work with in her artwork. Never one to let grass grow under her feet, Jill is currently off on another adventure - she is currently creating and publishing a line of cards, journals, prints, calendars and stationary items featuring her paper and collage designs for the gift market. Check www.tweetyjill.com for updates.

"I love anything old, aged and 'found' – which is why this year I produced a paper book called 'Scrapbook and Collage Papers ~ The European Collection'". The book is jam-packed with a breathtaking selection of designed papers, French script and Italian documents found on her travels to Europe, as well as vintage ephemera acquired over the years from local antique stores and flea markets.

Hunting for these kinds of finds is her idea of great fun, just as much as incorporating them into her art. She relishes spending a day going from antique stores to flea markets to large estate and garage sales. Some of the treasures she keeps an eye out for creating her art include vintage books, postage stamps, postcards, ephemera and old letters.

For her studio décor and storage she seeks out old colored glass vases and bowls in ruby reds, all shades of greens and deep blues, hat pins, baskets with character, china cups and bowls with pink roses, and interestingly shaped clear or colored vintage jars and bottles to store her studio stash of trims, lace, ribbons and embellishments. "One of the most enjoyable things about having a personal art studio," she reveals, "is decorating it with all your favorite things."

Hers most certainly include works – many of them gifts – from talented artistic friends such as Lesley Riley, KC Willis, Claudine Hellmuth, Roben-Marie Smith, Amy Wellenstein, Lisa Engelbrecht and others. The walls and shelves of her studio are lined with treasures and artwork, making an indelible mark and infusing even more personality into Jill's unusual work space. Each meaningful item reflects the special people in her life, right down to the cup from which she sips her coffee.

"One of my most cherished keepsakes is my dear, late grandmother's coffee cup. I drink coffee from it every day! She was such a precious, loving soul and had a tremendous impact on my upbringing, as well as my life today, and it makes me think of her daily. Old things remind us of times past and give us a sense of tradition and comfort. The rarity of vintage-era items creates a sense of mystery and intrigue for me, and, I believe, for most of us."

JILL'S PUBLICATIONS INCLUDE:
The Complete Guide to Scrapbooking
The Idea Book to Scrapbooking
Scrapbooking for Kids (Ages 1-100)
Scrapbooking as a Learning Tool
Vintage Collage for Scrapbooking
Creating Vintage Cards
Artists Creating with Photos
Making Cards with Rubber Stamps, Ribbons and Buttons
Shabby and Beyond Scrapbooking Ideas
Great Gifts Using Scrapbook Materials
Rubber Stamped Artists Trading Cards (ATCs)
Scrapbook & Collage Papers~ The European Collection (12"x12" double-sided acid free papers)
Altered! Art Projects
Creating with Fabric

BOOKS TO COME:
Fresh Techniques in Rubber Stamping
Altered, Altered & More Altered
Scrapbook & Collage Papers ~ The Designer Collection (12"x12" double-sided acid free papers)
Painting ~ Wood, Metal & Paper Mache

The Queen of Everything
~ Jill Haglund ~

MATERIALS

FABRICS: Coffee-Dyed Fabric; White and Off-White Color Plus Printable Fabrics by ColorTextiles; Various Fabrics; Wonder Under by Pellon

PAPERS: Music from Scrapbook & Collage Papers ~ The French Collection by TweetyJill Publications

ADHESIVES: Sobo Fabric Glue by Delta

OTHER: Pillow Form; Tulle; Batting (optional); Vintage Buttons; Crown Pin; Thread; Hand-Dyed Trim and Coffee-Dyed Doily; Quote; Scanned and Printed Vintage Photo or Vintage Postcard

TOOLS: Scissors; Pinking Shears (optional); Tape Measure; Needle; Pins; Photo-Editing Software; Iron

PRINTER: Epson CX6000 or Epson C88 Printer with DURABrite Inks

INSTRUCTIONS

1. Select all fabrics. Cut main fabric for front and back panels to fit over pillow form. Add one inch for seam allowance.

2. Coffee-dye desired trims; doily and fabric, dry and press to flatten.

3. Scan and print vintage postcard, as well as the music page from TweetyJill Publications' Scrapbook & Collage Papers ~ The French Collection, onto off-white printable fabric.

4. Collect and print a variety of quotes on white printable fabric to have on hand.

5. Position tulle on pillow front and tack with Sobo Fabric Glue. Let dry 20 minutes.

6. Cut Wonder Under to fit fabric pieces you plan to layer, following manufacturer's instructions to adhere to pillow.

8. Once adhered, decorate pillow by stitching around edges of all fabrics as shown, adjusting pattern width and length of stitches, as desired.

9. Sandwich batting in between photo and Wonder Under. Adhere to decorated panel. Repeat with quote. Sew edges to secure.

10. Hand-sew on vintage buttons. Attach crown pin.

11. Use Sobo Fabric Glue to adhere trims. Let dry 20 minutes. Sew trims to secure to pillow front with wide zigzag stitch.

12. Place decorated sides together and sew one inch from outside edge all the way around; leave a opening to insert pillow form.

13. Turn pillow shape inside out; push four corners to points and iron flat. Insert pillow through opening.

14. Pin open side; hand-sew to close with needle and thread.

Mary Engelbreit, Founder and Editor-in-Chief of Mary Engelbreit's Home Companion, has always has been a great source of inspiration to me. What a wonderful experience it was to actually meet her in person! It was during a signing of her new book, "Artful Words, Mary Engelbreit and the Illustrated Quote", at the Craft and Hobby International Trade Show last year in Anaheim, California. She is even more delightful then I imagined! I have always held her in the highest regard due to her skill, accomplishments in publishing, licensing of her illustrations and her perseverance in the artistic venue. After meeting her, I decided I wanted to create a little something personal to send to her to say thank you for all she gives. So I made her a pillow with one of her quotes! ~ Jill Haglund

Jill meets Mary Engelbreit at Mary's book signing

Queen of Everything.
—Mary Engelbreit

Codi's Birthday Pillow

Jill Haglund

Inspired by Lesley Riley's "Fragment Series".
Photo image from her CD Collection "Steppin' Out".

MATERIALS

FABRICS: Various Fabrics; Color Plus Fabrics by ColorTextiles; Batting; Wonder Under by Pellon

PAINTS: Fluid Acrylic Quinacridone/Nickel Azo Gold by Golden

ADHESIVES: Fabric Glue

OTHER: Scanned Photo or images on CDs from www.LaLasLand.com by Lesley Riley or www.Lunagirl.com by SummertownSun Publishing, LLC; Water; Desired Size Foam Pillow; Vintage Buttons;

TOOLS: Singer Sewing Machine; Paintbrush; Scissors; Pins

PRINTER: Epson C88 or CX 5000 with DURABrite Inks

INSTRUCTIONS

1. Select a favorite scanned image and quote or chose from CD Collections under Materials list. Print onto Color Plus Printable fabric.

2. For pillow front and back panels, cut two pieces the size of the pillow form, plus one inch, allowing for seam allowance. For decoration of panels, cut several favorite colors and patterns of fabric swatches to various sizes; juxtapose and layer pieces until you are pleased. Follow manufacturer's instructions to iron Wonder Under to fabric swatches; position and adhere onto pillow panels. Once in place, sew edges of all fabric pieces.

3. Mix a small amount of water with Fluid Acrylic Quinacridone/Nickel Azo Gold paint to age the image printed onto fabric. Apply a small amount with a paintbrush or your finger. You may want to practice first on a snippet of fabric.

4. Adhere aged photo and quote with Wonder Under. Sew around edges.

5. Sew coordinating fabric pieces to pillow.

6. Hand-sew vintage buttons on front and back of pillow panels.

7. With decorated pillow panels together, sew around edge, leaving an opening to turn pillow casing inside out.

8. Turn pillow casing inside out; stuff in pillow.

9. Pin open side and hand-sew closed with needle and thread.

STEP ONE

Using paper-backed fabric prepared for inkjet printing (ColorTextiles, EQ Printables), follow manufacturer's instructions and print image and quote onto fabric. After your photo is printed onto fabric, mix Quinacridone Gold Fluid Acrylic with water in a small bowl to create a diluted wash. Paint onto photo in small areas or around edge to age.

STEP TWO

Peel back adhesive from printed photo image and iron on Wonder Under. Layer all prepared fabrics and the aged photo to pillow panel(s) using Wonder Under as an adhesive. Sew around edges of all pieces.

STEP THREE

Layer more fabric pieces as shown and add quote. Sew around all edges. Hand-sew vintage buttons on pillow for embellishment.

STEP FOUR

With decorated sides together, sew pillow casing, leaving a one-inch seam allowance and an opening to insert pillow. Pink edges.

STEP FIVE

Turn pillow casing inside out; push four corners to points and iron flat. Insert pillow form through opening inch space. Hand-sew opening shut with slip stitch.

STEP SIX

Back of finished pillow decorated with layered fabrics and buttons.

This pillow was made for my bubbly, sweet friend, Codi, for her birthday. Custom-made "just for her"; I knew she would enjoy it! I wanted to incorporate a bit of femininity, a personalized message, her favorite colors and a few beautiful buttons and flowers because she loves the outdoors and gardening. I love the old photo of the two little girls with party hats and a birthday cake in between them. Can you imagine anyone not treasuring a unique gift like this one made especially for them? Next time you have a special occasion that requires giving a gift, think of sewing up a pillow. Great for weddings, anniversaries, graduation and of course birthdays, including first day of birth (with baby's photo). If you don't have a photograph of the actual event or person, select a vintage photo or scan a vintage postcard that may represent the date or person in some fashion, as I did on Codi's pillow.

I absolutely love collecting vintage buttons. I buy them on eBay, at garage sales, flea markets, antique stores, fabric or craft shops and wherever I can find them. I have many given to me as gifts because everyone knows I treasure them due to the vintage jars filled to the brim sitting around my studio. They are the perfect embellishments, not only for fragments, but for all fabric projects. ~ Jill Haglund

I still thoroughly enjoy nature in the form of flowers and birds; especially songbirds. My favorite "morning wake up call" is nature's song right outside my window.
~ Jill Haglund

Blue Jay Collage Pillow

❧ Jill Haglund ❧

MATERIALS

FABRICS: Hand-Dyed Metallic Coated Fabric; White and Off-White Printable Color Plus Fabrics by ColorTextiles; Wonder Under by Pellon

PAINTS: Gold Fluid Acrylic by Golden

PAPERS: Music and Marbled Papers from Scrapbook & Collage Papers ~ The French Collection by TweetyJill Publications

ADHESIVES: Sobo Fabric Glue by Delta

OTHER: Non-Copyrighted Images (or your own collage work); Pillow Form; Batting (optional); Vintage Button; Velvet Leaves; Thread; Tape Measure; Ephemera for Collage; Coffee-Dyed Trim; Hand-Dyed Ribbon by Lori Scott

TOOLS: Stencils; Scissors; Pinking Shears (optional); Pins; Iron

PRINTER: Epson CX6000 Printer with DURABrite Inks

INSTRUCTIONS

1. Select all fabrics. Cut main fabric for front and back panels to fit pillow form, adding one inch for seam allowance.

2. Coffee-dye desired trim; dry and press to flatten.

3. Create a collage using your ephemera and non-copyrighted images, along with papers and images from TweetyJill Publications Scrapbook & Collage Papers ~ The French Collection.

4. Stencil scroll pattern in gold acrylic onto purple fabric as shown. Pull threads on fabric to fray to create color and texture. Tack onto pillow front panel with Sobo Fabric Glue.

5. Scan and print music from TweetyJill Publications Scrapbook & Collage Papers ~ The French Collection onto off-white Color Plus fabric sheet. Repeat process with bird collage.

6. Cut and iron on Wonder Under to fit printed collage and music, following manufacturer's instructions to adhere. Using Wonder Under again, sandwich in a piece of batting cut slightly smaller then printed collage transfer; layer to front panel.

7. Once completed, secure all fabrics by sewing with decorative stitching as shown, adjusting pattern width and length of stitches as desired.

8. Stitch leaves and hand-sew a vintage flower button to pillow front.

9. Use Sobo Fabric Glue to adhere trims to front panel. Let dry 20 minutes. Sew coffee-dyed wide lace trim to bottom of front panel using wide zigzag stitch.

10. Secure ribbon by folding in half and sewing mid-section to top-left corner; tie in a bow and sew trailing ribbon pieces to pillow, framing collage as shown.

11. Place decorated sides together and sew one inch from outside edge all the way around; leave an eight-inch space unsewn. Pink edges.

12. Turn pillow shape inside out; push four corners to points and iron flat. Insert pillow through eight-inch space.

13. Pin open side; hand-sew closed with needle and thread.

My dad inspired my love of nature. Every time I visited him we would walk around his big yard admiring whatever new fruit trees and flowers he had planted; he could make that excursion around the yard last an hour. These are some of my fondest memories of him. ~ Jill Haglund

My daughter Lindsay is always tickled pink when she receives a handmade gift from me, which naturally gives me much enjoyment and enthusiasm when creating something meaningful for her. Although I gave this to her when she was 23, I used this photo I just love of her when she was about five, because it shows the essence of who she was then and who she continues to be - a free spirit, full of energy, life and sweetness! I chose green gingham since green has always been her favorite color, and of course, floral patterns because what girl at any age is not fond of flowers? ~ Jill Haglund

One of the greatest gifts I've ever gotten is my daughter Lindsay. ~Mama

My Daughter, Lindsay

❧ Jill Haglund ❧

MATERIALS

FABRICS: Green Cotton Gingham; Floral Fabrics; Tulle; Batting; White and Off-White Printed Color Plus Fabrics by ColorTextiles; Wonder Under by Pellon

ADHESIVES: Sobo Fabric Glue by Delta

OTHER: Pillow Form; Vintage Buttons; Thread; Personal Photo; Quote(s)

TOOLS: Scissors; Pinking Shears (optional); Iron; Needle; Pins; Measuring Tape

PRINTER: Epson CX6000 or C88 Printer with DURABrite Inks (color saturates fabric well)

INSTRUCTIONS

1. Select all fabrics. Measure and cut main fabric for front and back panels, depending on size of pillow form. Measure pillow and add one inch for seam allowance when sewing together.

2. Scan and print a personal photo and chosen quotes onto white printable fabric.

3. Glue a floral fabric strip diagonally across pillow front.

4. Position loosely-knotted tulle strips; tack with Sobo Fabric Glue. Let dry 20 minutes.

5. Cut Wonder Under to fit all fabric pieces and quotes.

6. Follow manufacturer's instructions to adhere Wonder Under to all decorative fabric pieces and adhere to front and back as desired.

7. Once adhered, decorate pillow by stitching around edges of all fabric pieces as shown, adjusting pattern width and length of stitches, as desired.

8. Sandwich batting in between photo and Wonder Under; iron to adhere to pillow. Sew around edge of photo to secure.

9. Sew quotes to pillow (front and back) as shown.

10. Hand-sew on vintage buttons as shown. (Optional: sew buttons onto back if desired.)

11. Place decorated sides together and sew one inch from outside edge all the way around; leave an opening to insert pillow. Pink edges to keep from fraying.

12. Turn pillow shape inside out; push four corners to points and iron flat. Insert pillow through opening.

13. Pin open side; hand-sew closed with needle and thread.

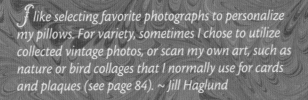

I like selecting favorite photographs to personalize my pillows. For variety, sometimes I chose to utilize collected vintage photos, or scan my own art, such as nature or bird collages that I normally use for cards and plaques (see page 84). ~ Jill Haglund

Alice's hands are folded in front of her as she walks up the path to view the garden and the sunset...

I created this Fragment Story (also called a "Story Quilt") in a class by Lesley Riley at Art & Soul in Portland, Oregon. I was motivated to move into fabric arts by Lesley and her teaching, as well as encouraged over the years by her fabulous work. ~ Jill Haglund

Alice in Wonderland

❧ Jill Haglund ❧

MATERIALS

FABRICS: Lightweight White Cotton; Patterned Fabrics (various textures, colors and weights); Wonder Under by Pellon

PAINTS: Fluid Acrylics by Golden

MARKERS / PENS: Micron Pigma Pen .08 Dark Brown by Sakura of America

ADHESIVES: Sobo Fabric Glue by Delta or Hot Glue Adhesive

OTHER: Velvet Leaves and Flowers; Wisp of Doll Hair; Ribbon; Felt (for hat); Hat Embellishment

TOOLS: Good, Sharp Fabric Scissors; Foam Brush; Hot Glue Gun

INSTRUCTIONS

1. Paint background loosely with acrylic paints and water for a wash of sunset.

2. Iron on Wonder Under to all fabrics except sheers. Once Wonder Under is ironed onto fabrics, begin to cut out pieces; tree with limbs and branches; fabric leaves for tree; fabric to create hill.

3. Select sheer fabric for skirt and top. Cut out each piece separately and shape as desired, keeping blousy. Work into shapes with flowing folds; sew a gather at the top of the skirt and stitch or glue to hold.

NOTE: Do not adhere Wonder Under to sheer dress fabric. Stitch or glue edges of sheer fabric you want to leave full and blousy. Wonder Under only works when you want to iron fabrics flat onto another fabric.

4. Make blouse using the same technique. Cut a basic body shape and hand-sew or glue to base. Adhere skirt onto bodice with Sobo Fabric Glue or a hot glue gun. Her blouse is cut to make it appear as if her hands are folded in front of her. Glue or stitch on a ribbon for a belt; tie in a bow.

5. Create felt hat. Glue hair under hat with glue gun. Add embellishment to hat. Position hat on Alice's head so it appears she is walking with her back to the viewer and headed up the hill.

6. Glue on the velvet leaves and flowers with Sobo Fabric Glue or hot glue gun.

7. Once dry, write your story. Frame if desired.

My inspiration for this comes from one of my favorite childhood books, "Alice in Wonderland". I actually own a vintage copy printed in 1953. I remember being fascinated by the intricate, detailed illustrations exacting the story lines. I still love looking at the rabbit with his pocket watch in his hand afraid to be "late for a very important date", the queen, the card people and so many more. But what stands out is Alice. I have read the book many times and I love certain passages. One is used as a starter for my Journal Quilt... "You can see the garden much better if you walk up the path". Because my grandmother and her garden always stay so dear to my heart, I finished the story with her in mind... she taught me the names of all the flowers in her beautiful garden when I was a little girl.

~ Jill Haglund

Pamela Allen
aka
PaminCan

CHAPTER 12

Pamela Allen

"I do quilts about women that are chubby, who are no longer babes. My work celebrates middle-age as opposed to the negative images we see on TV. People appreciate it because that's their life too. We are wiser and deeper and more interested in the humanness of life than in the clothes and beer and boys of our youth."

Pamela Allen is one hot mama. Literally. Having achieved status as "a woman of a certain age" she says, "I enjoy getting older, but these hot flashes! Everything else is fine – I haven't become a crabby old lady, I'm just hot!" The globally-lauded art quilter has both a sense of humor and an appreciation of the mature woman, a recurring theme in her work. Among many award-winning quilts, "One Hot Mama" depicts a robust-looking lady trying to cool down with both hand-held and electrical fans.

Pamela is a mama by marriage; her husband had six children. "We have an unusual family – I was a lab technologist up to the age of 30 – but couldn't see myself doing that all my life, so I enrolled in art school. That's how I met my hus-band - he was my painting professor. He's 21 years older, so at 58 I already have grand and great grandchildren." Fifteen, actually, and they are the inspiration for her pieces, "Childless Grandmother" and "Grandmother's Lullaby" - "It's of me, the generic grandmother, singing to a generic grandchild on my lap!"

Her work spans other themes as well. With a Bachelor's Degree in Fine Arts from Queen's University in her native Canada, she began her career as a paint-er, exploring the theme of "the child in all of us." After 20 years of what she modestly terms "making a small ripple in my local pond" she transitioned to fabric art – and became internationally famous. "I was just amazed at the me-teoric rise in sales and the recognition factor. I was puzzled, why? Maybe it's because it has an integrity to it, a joie de vivre - and the fabric medium suits me down to the ground.

Pamela has exhibited in the United States, France and Japan as well as Canada. She addition-ally maintains an ambitious schedule of workshops that also keep her traveling, one of her favorite things to do. Trips to Europe, Mexico and particularly the South-western United States have all nurtured her penchant for bright color and folk imagery. "Every time we go, new things percolate through my visual memory bank. I really clicked with the flavor of Native American and Latino art because of the colors. Here in Canada we're just cold and gray; there, it's warm and expansive. And there's so much history." Another strong influence has been her work with children, as she has participated in more than ten Artists in the Schools grants funded by the Ontario Arts Council.

Despite her busy schedule, she turns out about 20-30 beautifully intricate pieces a year, winning prestigious awards too numerous to mention. Her work incorporates recycled fabrics ("they have their own history") and a stash of unexpected embellishments. "I like safety pins, bobbins, Christmas lights, little tiny violins, keys and jingle bells (because I like the quilt to sing). I like to implement unusual things in my work. Some are downright tacky! I will use plastic eggs around a female's stomach to represent fertility and styrofoam fruit for breasts. Garters are universal symbols. A lot of women think they're hilarious, and thank God we no longer have to use them!"

After 22 years of working in a separate studio, she converted the entire third floor of her home to create her vibrant fabric art. "I have a sort of puritan work ethic; I work Monday through Friday, 9-5. I have several pieces going on at once - I like to stagger them so I can take the hand-work downstairs and watch the telly with my hubby. I'm really fortunate that he is also an artist because he understands what's going on in my head and I understand what's going on in his."

It takes Pamela about three weeks to complete a large piece, and about ten days for a smaller one, although she teaches a workshop where six are created in one day! When she first forayed into fabric art, she didn't even know how to sew. "I started throwing things together, hand-sewing. Then got a clunky old sewing machine, it cost $30. I had to duct tape the feed dogs! I would go to thrift shops and get hideous bridesmaid dresses to cut up – so I had a pitiful stash and a pitiful machine!"

Now she encourages her students to focus on the

basic elements of art and design rather than sewing and technique. "I've noticed over time a lot of quilters feel compelled to make templates. So I give them assignments that will liberate them from this. We'll concentrate on a single design element, such as choosing a color scheme. Then I'll tell them they can do anything they like, but it must include a fish or a glass of wine. I look at my watch (dramatically) and say 'You've got 30 minutes.' It's amazing to see what they do once they get used to the time frame. They love it! They really enjoy breaking out of the box."

Pamela's own work is totally spontaneous. "I just start throwing fabric together and it just becomes something in the making. My images are drawn from events and relationships in my own life. These seem to strike a chord universally." Just a glance at her website, http://pamelart2.homestead.com/quiltythings.html, reveals a fascinating patchwork of themes. And whether it's a fabric postcard, journal quilt or wall hanging… if it's a "Pamela Allen", people recognize it. "I work as a painter would work. My techniques aren't as important to me. My main focus is the message, the composition... scale, design, color, contrast. And my subject matter is so different from anyone else's. It's very exciting for me as an artist to find my niche.

If days go by and I haven't worked I get very antsy. I want to get back to what I call my 'real purpose in life.' We make starts at our careers and then the art sort of nags at you from the inside, because that's what you truly want to do. Making art is not the most lucrative job in the world, but you can learn to live with a lot less when you love going to work each day.

allen5@sympatico.ca

PaminCan

I usually start a project with only a vague idea. Frequently the jumping off point will be the fabrics I have on hand, rather than a clear idea of the subject.

I have what other quilters think is a pathetically small stash, as I use a lot of recycled fabrics from thrift shops and rarely buy yardage at fabric stores. Therefore my turnover in available fabrics is rapid, but on the other hand, I always have new and unlikely materials to choose from.

In this case, I had some dress remnants as well as silk fabric meant for upholstery. The latter two were given to me by a fellow fabric artist, no doubt taking pity on me!

I had been looking at medieval manuscript illuminations recently so I knew I wanted to borrow some elements like rich color, pattern and decoration.

STEP-BY-STEP OF PAMELA'S VERY STINGY TOOTH FAIRY QUILT:

STEP ONE

Start each project by constructing a full quilt sandwich... back, batting, and top. First, make a background out of several fabrics to create some sort of space; avoid the look of a flat backdrop. Begin building the composition by cutting fabric shapes and finding interesting combinations (see detail) to form the figure.

Apart from setting the placement of the figure in the space, I have no clear idea as yet about the objects in the composition.

STEP TWO

All that is defined composition-wise at this point is the basic background and that the wings frame the corner and the figure is asymmetrically placed.

STEP THREE

Once satisfied, spray-baste all the elements down and begin hand-appliqué with embroidery floss and a big ladder stitch. Stitch through both the front layer and the batting, but not the back at this point. This introduces a line to the composition as well as color, and begins to add a puffy texture that I like in my work.

Close up detail of tooth fairy and the background positioned and pinned to quilt.

As I am stitching, I am thinking about what can come next, and in this case, I decide the figure is not to be an angel, but a fairy! In fact, a TOOTH fairy, which seems appropriate, as I recently broke a front tooth!

Close up detail of the tooth fairy quilt - all shapes and background are positioned and sewn down.

STEP FOUR

The shapes are stitched with embroidery floss. By choosing blue and green stitching in the lower part of the composition, the eye travels from those same colors to elsewhere in the picture.

I have now got a much clearer idea of what will be going on in the piece. I know I have some relevant embellishment that will be put on later as well as symbols that I will be quilting in the background. I prepare for the quilting by simply outlining the major features in order to stabilize the whole thing.

Close up detail-sewn

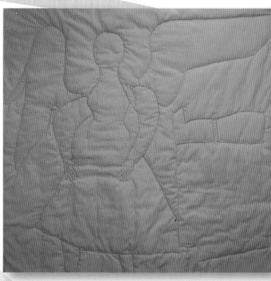

back

STEP FIVE

Add additional shapes to tell a story.

Having decided on the subject, I can now begin to add elements that tell my story. I patch together fabric shapes to form a bed, thinking I can have the scenario of the fairy exchanging the tooth for some coins. I try to create visual unity by choosing fabrics similar to the original figure, and in some cases - as in the heavy egg-shaped upholstery fabric – identical, so as to lead the eye around the whole composition. I have also given the poor thing a head!

The quilting is all done except for a few areas where I might tweak it after blocking. I leave some areas relatively unstitched as I want to emphasize the torso of the figure as well as the puffiness of the bed pillows.

Close up detail of the bed's fabric shapes pinned in place on the left.

STEP SIX
EMBELLISHMENTS:

Sometimes my quilting is influenced by what I have decided to use as embellishment. In this case, I know I will be applying dental mirrors as a corona, so I quilt in a kind of halo that will feature it. I now know I will be adding purely decorative elements too, in keeping with the medieval imagery. Thus, much of the quilting is also decorative. I add a meandering flower to give some imagery to the right side of the work.

STEP SEVEN
BLOCKING:

I learned through experience that the work must be blocked before I square it up and put on the binding. I use a plant mister to soak the back of the quilt evenly and pin it as flat and square as possible to my cork topped cutting table. (see photo of studio). Depending on time constraints, I either use a fan on it or let it dry overnight.

STEP EIGHT
LASER LEVEL:

I then use my cross hair laser level to square the piece. This tool has become a mainstay in my ongoing attempts to improve my quilting technique. In the early days of my fabric art, I paid no attention to such things and consequently was an embarrassment to myself for the "wonkiness" of my hangings! The same was true of my pathetic early bindings where I used to simply fold the backing to the front and somehow try to stitch it neatly… - NOT! These days, I make a separate and acceptable binding for the edges of my work, thanks to a student who forced me to learn how simple and easy it was!

STEP NINE
BINDING:

Now I have my work square and ready to apply the binding. I audition several fabrics around the edges and decide I do not want the binding to be contrasting; I choose the light dotted fabric already present in the composition because I like the look of it blending in. To stabilize the edge, I first sew a 1/4" stay stitching all around the perimeter. Once the binding is sewn down, I decide to add a bit more quilting to even any bumps and bulges. I also sew a hanging sleeve onto the back as I have discovered that trying to sew it on *after* embellishing can be difficult.

95

I have a huge stash to choose from... dollar store items, flea market finds and yard sale doodads. A year ago, I was sent a box of dental mirrors of all things, by a cyber friend who happened to be a dental assistant. Finally, I get to use them! They make a perfect halo for a tooth fairy. I add lots of beads, upholstery fringe, cording, ribbon and fancy buttons to enhance the feeling of a medieval illumination. I gold-leaf two little boxes and glue a tooth in one (don't worry, it's a model plastic tooth I got from my dentist!) and a Canadian five-cent piece in the other. That suggested the perfect title, thus THE STINGY TOOTH FAIRY is complete. ~ Pamela Allen

WEEPING WOMAN

My mother became suddenly and critically ill in 2005. My sister and I were
at her ICU bedside for 16 days while doctors went to extreme measures promising
she would recover. I weep because she died after all her suffering on the 17th day.
I am reminded of the many weeping women Picasso did over his lifetime.
This gave me permission in a way, to be extremely literal in the rendition of tears.
Bleeding hearts also behave as a decoration/emotional element around the neck.
This was my Journal entry for January 2005. ~ Pamela Allen

Gull Girl:

We had such frivolous issues in our youth. We were all "babes" once, strutting our firm, lithe bodies on the beach in bikinis and baby oil. Then something wonderful happens to women when we reach middle age. We can relax, enjoy our ripe roundness, wear a sensible bathing suit and commune with the surf, sand and seabirds. ~ Pamela Allen

Ducks in a Row

2005 was a challenging year for me. My Mother died suddenly, my sister was diagnosed with cancer (she is in remission now) and my husband's daughter died just before Christmas. I was strained and stressed on the day my little grandson gave me his adorable drawing of a duck. I realized there was still much to be thankful for and it was time to get my personal ducks in a row. I enlarged Dexter's drawing and made a template for my row of quackers. There are some references to grieving in the weeping willow tree and the rain falling, just as one sees in 19th century mourning samplers. Nevertheless, doing the quilt was a wonderful consolation and symbol for me of a hopeful future. ~ Pamela Allen

COLD CANADIANS

This quilt was in a special exhibition at the Patchwork Expo in Lyon, France in 2006. The theme, "Culture of my Country" was to give the artist the opportunity to showcase her country's particular character. I wanted to avoid the obvious like Mounties and the inevitable subject of cold Canadian winters. It took centuries for European colonizers to finally believe what our native Inuit people knew all along... that is, that the parka is the ideal garment for our frigid winters.
I paid homage to Inuit art by quilting in some well-known symbols of their culture, such as migrating caribou, snowy owl, Canada geese and salmon. Recycled velvets and rayon were perfect fabrics for the dense trapunto-like quilting.
~ Pamela Allen

Detail of back of Cold Canadians

ONE HOT MAMA

For the most part, I enjoy being middle-aged. No more worries about looking thin and terrific all the time.
A lot of wisdom gathered over the years. Many grandchildren to love. Comfortable friends who have ripened
along with me. But one very annoying consequence are those hot flashes that are the signature of a
"woman of a certain age" I feel like a walking five-alarm fire, and will go nowhere without my trusty fan.
So I HAD to make a quilt about it, complete with fans, firedogs and engines and hot, hot color.
~ Pamela Allen

Detail of Red Hot Mama: Notice the sewn fire truck in the background >

GRANDMOTHER'S LULLABY

I have no children of my own. But I was lucky to marry a man with six grown-up children, and in the last 25 years they have given me 15 grandchildren! I got to cuddle, sing to and love these children, so I thought a quilt about them was in order. I created a "generic" grandbaby to represent them all and quilted in the lyrics of the song... "I love you, a bushel and a peck." The grandmother is embellished with many symbols of woman... eggs for fertility, keys as the chatelaine, sewing gear as the mender, clothespegs as the laundress, and oh my gosh! Remember garters? ~ Pamela Allen

CATCH OF THE DAY- CARP DIEM

I am a member of an online quilt art group. In 2005, we held exhibition in Pueblo Colorado the theme of which was "Carpe Diem" or seize the day. I was uninspired by the theme and bent on a little mischief, so I did this quilt as a visual pun on the theme. Carp (fish) became the catch of the day (diem)! I was able to make a nice table setting with a real fork, spoon and napkin. I often use recycled fabrics and in this case I used sumptuous velvets and tafetta from those hideous bridesmaid dresses you can find in thrift shops. Carp is not the most delicate fish, so mine is enhanced with beads, and embossing to make him more appetizing. ~ Pamela Allen

Black-Eyed Susans with Fruit

I had just seen the Gees Bend quilts in Orlando and was struck by the improvisational character of the work. The irregularities and the obvious hand of the artists made them look very much like paintings. So I set myself the challenge of doing my flower quilt in a very loose style, with found scrap materials and an attitude of anything goes!
~ Pamela Allen

Funky Fiddler

I had found some tiny little violins and violas at the Dollar Store and wanted to use them as embellishment. But they sat in a bin for many months, until one evening when I was watching a special concert of the Scottish Fiddle Orchestra on TV. There, in close-up, was a wonderfully lively bass player - a very round and ripe woman - who was playing her heart out with great abandon. Thus, Funky Fiddlers was conceived. I was struck by the similarities between the violin and the shape of a woman's body, so my fiddlers are as curvaceous as their instruments. The quilting has related imagery in the form of the violin's scrolled neck and pegs, pan pipes, some brass instruments and the decorative "f" hole of a violin. Luckily I found some wooden musical notes at the aforementioned Dollar Store which made perfect embellishments. Oh, I never DID find a place for the original tiny violins!

~ Pamela Allen

FOUR WOMEN LAUGHING

A group of fiber artists met in Florida this spring and this
commemorates the four of us who worked and played and
wined and laughed together. ~ Pamela Allen

GUINEA FOWL

Whenever we vacation in Myrtle Beach, we shop at a particular supermarket for the sole reason that the manager keeps tame Guinea fowls in the parking lot. These are beautifully smooth-feathered birds and quite fun to watch. I finally was inspired to make a quilt about them... and confess I used some West African tribal flags as a resource for the image of the birds! ~ Pamela Allen

Gone Fish'in

When I was a child, some of the happiest
times were when I went fishing. My sister
was unlikely to impale some poor defenseless
worm on a hook, so I always went by myself.
Oh, the thrill of feeling a nibble! But even better
was bringing home a string of perch.
~ Pamela Allen

Below: Detail of Back Side of Hen Party Quilt

Hen Party

Compared to most art quilters, I have a pitifully small stash. Many
of my colleagues know this and more than once I have received a box of fabrics
from generous cyber friends right out of the blue. This quilt is made entirely from
a gift box in colors I would not normally have chosen.... burgundy, orange, yellow...
and furthermore, they were mostly cut into little 4" squares! Definitely from a
traditional patchwork quilter to one who couldn't piece anything to save her life.
So I just overlapped similarly colored squares to make a larger background and
constructed a very long-necked lady with a checkered bodice. Sometimes, when I
get to this stage I have to invent a scenario to form some kind of narrative.
I put a chicken roosting on her arm... then quilted in a number of other chickens.
Voila! The Hen Party. ◢ *Pamela Allen*

SNAKE CHARMER

*I hate vacuuming. The machine is heavy and noisy and the house needs cleaning again in a week's time anyway.
I want to conjure up a magical Hoover that does my bidding like a snake does for a charmer.*
~ *Pamela Allen*

Product Resource Guide

Anita's Art Stamps: Local Craft Store

Artful Scrapbooking & Rubber Stamps:
www.artfulscrapbook.com

Avery: www.avery.com

BasicGrey: www.basicgrey.com

Bazzill Basics Paper: www.bazzillbasics.com

Bernina USA: www.berninausa.com

Character Constructions:
www.characterconstructions.com

Clearsnap, Inc.:
www.clearsnap.com

Color Textiles, Inc.:
www.colortextiles.com

Daler-Rowney:
www.daler-rowney.com

Darlene Troyer:
www.magdalenamoon.com

Delta:
www.deltacrafts.com

DMC:
www.dmc-usa.com

Duncan Enterprises:
www.duncancrafts.com

Electric Quilt: www.electricquilt.com

Embellishment Village: www.embellishmentvillage.com

Epson: www.epson.com

Faber-Castell USA: www.faber-castellusa.com

Gane Brothers & Lane, Inc.: www.ganebrothers.com

Gingher: www.gingher.com

Golden Artist Colors, Inc.: www.goldenpaints.com

Gutermann: www.gutermann.com

Hero Arts: www.heroarts.com

HP: www.hewlettpackard.com

Husqvarna Viking: www.husqvarnaviking.com

Jacquard Products:
www.jacquardproducts.com

Janome America, Inc.: www.janome.com

John Neal Booksellar:
www.johnnealbooks.com

June Tailor: www.junetailor.com

K&Company:
www.kandcompany.com

LaLas Land:
www.lalasland.com

Lesley Riley:
www.lalasland.com

Lipstick Ranch: www.lipstickranch.com

Lisa Engelbrecht: www.lisaengelbrecht.com

Lorri Scott: www.lasfibers.com

Magdalena Moon: www.magdalenamoon.com

Magic Threads: www.magicthreads.com

Making Memories: www.makingmemories.com

Midori Ribbons: www.midoriribbons.com

Moda: www.modafabrics.com

OTT-LITE: www.ottlite.com

Pellon: www.shoppellon.com

Portfolio Series: www.portfolioseries.com

Provo Craft: www.provocraft.com

Prym-Dritz: www.dritz.com

Quilty Things:
http://pamelart2.homestead.com/tythings.html

Quilters Resource: www.quiltersresource.com

Ranger Industries, Inc.: www.rangerink.com

Rowenta: www.rowentausa.com

Sakura of America:
www.sakuraofamerica.com

Sears: www.sears.com

Sharpie: www.sharpie.com

Staedtler: www.staedtler-usa.com

SummertownSun Publishing, LLC:
www.summertownsun.com

Teemie's Blooms: www.teemiesblooms.com

The Thread Gatherer: www.threadgatherer.com

The Warm Company: www.warmcompany.com

Tombow: www.tombowusa.com

TweetyJill Publications: www.tweetyjill.com

USArtQuest, Inc.: www.usartquest.com